PENGUIN

YOUNG THOMAS HARDY

Robert Gittings was born in Portsmouth in 1911, the son of a naval surgeon. He was educated at St Edward's School, Oxford, and Jesus College, Cambridge, where he was Scholar, Research Student, and then Fellow and Supervisor of Studies.

Between 1940 and 1963, Dr Gittings was a producer and writer of features and educational scripts for the B.B.C. Since then, he has been a Visiting Professor at several universities in the U.S.A. He has had many volumes of his own verse and verse dramas published over the past forty years. His *Collected Poems* appeared in 1976.

Robert Gittings has received many literary and academic awards, including the Annual Award of the Royal Society of Literature in 1955. It is for his biography *John Keats*, however, that the greatest recognition has come. It won him the W. H. Smith Literary Award for 'the most outstanding contribution to English Literature' published in 1968, and was unanimously applauded by the critics. He also won the Christian Gauss Award of Phi Beta Kappa in 1975 for *Young Thomas Hardy*.

Young Thomas Hardy

Robert Gittings

PENGUIN BOOKS

Penguin Books Ltd, Harmondsworth, Middlesex, England
Penguin Books, 625 Madison Avenue, New York, New York 10022, U.S.A.
Penguin Books Australia Ltd, Ringwood, Victoria, Australia
Penguin Books Canada Ltd, 2801 John Street, Markham, Ontario, Canada L3R 1B4
Penguin Books (N.Z.) Ltd, 182–190, Wairau Road, Auckland 10, New Zealand

—

First published by Heinemann Educational Books 1975

—

Published with revisions in Penguin Books 1978

—

Copyright © Robert Gittings, 1975

Made and printed in Great Britain by
Richard Clay (The Chaucer Press) Ltd, Bungay, Suffolk
Set in Linotype Lectura

ANNABELLA TO THE RESCUE

'Now!' she yelled

ANNABELLA
TO THE RESCUE

by

MARY FITT

Illustrated by Richard Kennedy

THOMAS NELSON AND SONS LTD
LONDON EDINBURGH PARIS MELBOURNE
TORONTO AND NEW YORK

THOMAS NELSON AND SONS LTD
Parkside Works Edinburgh 9
36 Park Street London W1
312 Flinders Street Melbourne C1
218 Grand Parade Centre   Cape Town

THOMAS NELSON AND SONS (CANADA) LTD
91–93 Wellington Street West   Toronto 1

THOMAS NELSON AND SONS
19 East 47th Street New York 17

SOCIÉTÉ FRANÇAISE D'EDITIONS NELSON
25 rue Henri Barbusse Paris Ve

———

First published 1955

Printed in Great Britain by
Thomas Nelson and Sons Ltd, Edinburgh

CONTENTS

LIST OF ILLUSTRATIONS

ANNABELLA TO THE RESCUE

CHAPTER 1

JOURNEY TO TREGLO

I

STRUCTURAL alterations were being done in Annabella's London school, so the school was closed, and the children were sent, after some delay, to other schools in different parts of the country—just like the evacuees during the War, as Daisy and Johnnie Green, Annabella's friends, told her. Annabella knew nothing about the War except what her parents had told her, and they had not told her much, because they lived in the Transvaal, South Africa, where Annabella was born, and they had not known much about the War.

Her father and mother were now travelling in the United States, and Annabella was staying in London with her Uncle Bob and Aunt Meg, where she was very happy.

When she heard that the school was to be closed, and that the children were to be sent away, if their parents agreed, to other schools, Annabella was sorry at first. Uncle Bob went to see the headmaster, Mr. Marley, and when he came back that evening to supper, he had some interesting news to report.

2

' Well, my dear,' he said to Aunt Meg as he sat down at the table and sniffed appreciatively as she cut the first slice of a steak-and-kidney pie, and the steam rose, ' I put your suggestion to Mr Marley, and he thinks it an excellent one.' He turned to look with a smile at Annabella, who had no idea what he meant, and was filled with impatient curiosity. ' Your Aunt Meg,' he said, ' has a cousin —a sort of cousin—called William Williams, who is the headmaster of the village school at Treglo, on the border between England and Wales.'

' Shall I be going to his school ? ' said Annabella, to whom a village school seemed rather a come-down after London.

' No, dear,' interposed Aunt Meg, ' You are too big for that. But there is a big Secondary Modern School quite near, and your Uncle Bob has been writing to my cousin Bill, and he says——'

' He says,' continued Uncle Bob, ' you couldn't get a better school anywhere. And he also suggests—he and his wife, who will soon, I hope, be as well known to you as your Aunt Meg——'

' A kinder woman than my cousin—or nearly cousin, Louise, never lived,' said Aunt Meg ; ' and she is a wonderful cook. Wait till you taste her apple dumplings.'

' I don't believe anybody is as nice as you, Aunt Meg,' said Annabella, or '—as she began to eat her steak-and-kidney pie—' a better cook.'

' I endorse that,' said Uncle Bob.

There was silence for a minute. Then Annabella said :

' *Where* did you say this place is, Uncle Bob ? '

' It's somewhere on the borders of England and Wales,' said Uncle Bob, ' and it's quite near a big coal-field. Some of our best coal comes from near there.'

' But won't it be awfully dirty ? ' said Annabella, ' and the people all black with coal-dust ? '

' I don't *think* so,' said Uncle Bob doubtfully. ' After all, the people don't *all* go down the mines. And your Uncle Bill says that the countryside is quite beautiful. I've never been there myself.'

' It is,' said Aunt Meg. ' I've been there. It's all mountains and rivers—and not far from the sea. And everywhere—inside the houses, for instance—it's quite clean. The air is lovely. And I said to my cousin-in-law, Louise Williams —I said, " *Your* curtains keep much cleaner than mine," and she said, " It's because the air's so *clean*." So you see, you'll love it. And it 'll be a change for you.'

'I don't want a change,' said Annabella. 'I don't *like* changes.'

3

Gradually it became clear that Uncle Bob had suggested that Annabella and several of her friends should be sent to Treglo, where they could be boarded out—Annabella with her aunt's cousin, and the others with other families in the village; and they could continue their education at the new Secondary Modern School at Melintre, two miles farther down the valley. Mr. Marley knew of the school, and he had found out that the headmaster would gladly take the new pupils from London; and so when all the arrangements had been made and the Education Authorities had been satisfied, that was how it was fixed.

But the Melintre School had room for only three pupils; and it was difficult to arrange to admit even these because the school, which had about six hundred scholars, always had a long waiting list, and of the children who were on this many were weeded out by the entrance examinations. It was proposed that the other two pupils, who were to accompany Annabella, should be chosen likewise by examination, but Annabella said she wouldn't go unless her friends Johnnie and Daisy came too, so Mr. Marley, who knew all three would do him credit, reserved the right to make his own choice ; and so it was that the three friends sat together one day in a third-class compartment rolling westwards.

Daisy said to her brother :

' D'you think we're going to like this, Johnnie ? '

Johnnie never accepted anything on trust. He said :

' I've no idea. But I fancy they'll all be savages down there. And everything will be as black as coal. It could be fun to be amongst savages for a time, and be black instead of white.'

Annabella repeated what Aunt Meg had said about the cleanliness.

' Oh, you're always an optimist ! ' said Johnnie, as if that were a very wrong, or at least a silly, thing to be.

' What's an optimist ? ' said Daisy.

' It's a person,' said Johnnie, ' who believes that—that everything is always for the best. The opposite is a pessimist.'

' What's that ? '

' A pessimist is a person who believes that everything is for the worst,' said Johnnie.

' And are you *that* ? ' said Annabella, shocked.

' Of course not,' said Johnnie scornfully. ' I keep an open mind.'

' What's that ? ' said Daisy, who was always

asking questions, though she didn't always listen to the answers.

'It means,' said Johnnie, 'I expect nothing, either good or bad. I just—wait and see.'

'Oh, how dull!' cried Annabella. But she herself was feeling a little nervous about what they would find at the other end.

Annabella had done part of this journey before, when she travelled westward; she even thought she recognised some of the fields and the farmhouses, but Johnnie laughed at the idea.

Annabella was annoyed, and this made her reckless; so when they ran into a tunnel she informed her friends:

'This is the Severn Tunnel; it takes seven and a half minutes to run through it.'

Johnnie looked at his wrist watch. But in a minute or two they ran into daylight again.

'Oh, I'm sorry,' said Annabella. 'I made a mistake. This is the first tunnel; I think it runs under the Cotswold Hills.'

Johnnie smiled, in a superior way he had, as if to say, 'That's what you say now.'

When they did actually reach the Severn Tunnel after they had passed Bristol Annabella said nothing, though she felt sure that this time they really were there. The banks on each side of the railway became higher and steeper, and soon they were in darkness, except for the yellow glimmer of the compartment lights. A queer smell filled the compartment, and the windows clouded over with some white substance.

A gentleman opposite who had been reading a newspaper got up and closed all the windows. The train ran slowly, and there were banging noises which, Johnnie said, were signals.

The gentleman opposite said :

' Children, you are now under the bed of one of the biggest rivers in Britain. The tunnel is nearly four and a half miles long, and it took thirteen years to build.' He leaned forward. ' I know, you see, because my grandfather and my father were members of the firm of engineers responsible. Hayshaw is the name. It was finished in 1886—the year I was born. You can imagine the difficulties,' he said, ' the engineers had when I tell you that at the lowest part—about where we are now— the depth of water above us at high tide is about a hundred feet.' He chuckled. ' That's a lot of water ! '

' Oh, dear ! ' said Daisy, looking anxiously at the windows as if she expected to see the water all round them just outside. At that moment something queer happened inside their ears, and the three children clapped their hands over their ears.

'It's the pressure,' said Mr. Hayshaw. 'It alters just here—where we are deepest—and affects your ear-drums. Don't be afraid; they'll come all right in a minute.'

And so they did, when the train ran safely and smoothly out at the other end. Mr. Hayshaw told them a few more facts about the Severn, and the Bristol Channel into which it runs. He said suddenly to Johnnie:

'Do you know what a *bore* is, my boy?'

Johnnie, with a superior smile, said:

'Yes, sir. A bore is a person who talks too much and tells you things you don't want to hear.'

'You're a smart lad, aren't you?' said Mr. Hayshaw, giving Johnnie a sharp look. 'But you don't get my meaning. I'm talking about a river bore, which probably you've never seen. They don't have them on the Thames, you know, for all their smartness. Now *I* live in a house which is built on a cliff, high over the Severn, and I've seen many a bore. . . . But you don't want to hear; you just know everything.'

Johnnie turned red, and Annabella, anxious to preserve the peace, said:

'Oh, please, do tell us!'

So Mr. Hayshaw told them about the bores in tidal rivers, and the Severn in particular, and how exciting they were to watch, and how destructive they could be; and this occupied them till they reached the station where they were to get out.

The children inquired about the train they were to take now—a small train on a branch line going up a valley. When they were seated in an empty carriage, Annabella said:

'Johnnie, you were very rude to Mr. Hayshaw; he knew quite well what you meant.'

Johnnie said nothing.

Annabella went on:

'*I* thought it was very interesting, what he said. I hope you're not going to be like that with all the new people we meet. If you are, we're going to be very unpopular. "When in Rome, do as the Romans do." '

'Well, you can if you like,' burst out Johnnie. 'But I'm not going to alter just to please a lot of strangers. I don't believe in currying favour. And anyhow, I knew what a tidal bore was, only I just didn't choose to say.'

Annabella and Daisy laughed.

4

The little train was now climbing up a valley with green fields on each side, and sloping hillsides. There were farms and cattle and sheep, and duckponds, and occasionally they passed over a level crossing. At one of them there was a school bus waiting, and a number of children, boys and girls, on bicycles. They wore school hats and blazers. A moment later the train stopped at a small station called MELINTRE. Here on the platform there was a crowd of girls and boys dressed like those at the level crossing.

Suddenly the train was filled. About a dozen boys and girls scrambled into the compartment, and threw their books, strapped together, on to the racks. They talked about things and people unknown to Annabella and Johnnie and Daisy, and at one moment they crowded over to the window and looked out. The train was now moving again. On the green hillside Annabella saw a long, low, red brick building with many windows. Round it were neat small trees, and gravel paths, and farther out, playing fields.

She gathered that this was the school they would soon be attending.

After quite a short run the train stopped at the next station; it was called Treglo. Annabella said :

'Come on ! We're here !' and she and Daisy and Johnnie got out on to a small winding platform that seemed to be surrounded with hills.

Three others, two girls and a boy, got out ;

they were from the school. They waved goodbye to their friends and the train went chugging away uphill until it soon disappeared round a curve.

One of the girls said :

' Are you by any chance Annabella Slade ? '

' Yes.'

' Then you're staying with us. My name's Theodora Williams, and this is my sister Julie. We were told to look out for you.'

They all shook hands, and Annabella introduced Daisy and Johnnie Green.

' Oh,' said Theodora, who was ' Theo ' for short, ' you're staying with Wilf.'

The boy with them, who was taller and bigger, came forward, hands in pockets, and looked them up and down.

' This is Wilf Stott,' said Theo. ' He's in the Fifth and he's——'

' Oh, shut up ! ' said Wilf.

Theo went on :

' He lives in the same street as we do. In fact,' she laughed, ' there's only one street in Treglo, as you'll see. There it is.'

They looked where she indicated, and saw a double row of houses running up the hillside. Annabella felt a little daunted.

' You're staying with *him*,' said Theo to Daisy and Johnnie, ' or rather, with his people.'

2

'Are you by any chance Annabella Slade?'

Johnnie was already looking sullen and angry, but Daisy said brightly :

' That 'll be nice.'

' It won't,' said Wilf.

' I meant,' persisted Daisy, ' it will be nice of you to have us.'

' It won't,' said Wilf again.   ' It has nothing to do with us. It was wished on us, by Mr. Williams,' and he glowered at Theo as if it were *her* fault. ' Well, come on, we may as well go home and get some tea.   I'm hungry.'

He turned and, somewhat to Annabella's surprise, Johnnie followed and of course Daisy. Annabella looked at Theo in dismay.

' Don't worry,' said Theo, laying a hand on Annabella's arm.   ' He's not a bad sort really. He's one of the kind that people mean when they say, " His bark's worse than his bite." '

' *I* hate dogs that bark,' said Annabella, ' with or without reason.   However . . .'

Theo and Julie took her one by each arm, and they went off together,   Theo said :

' Roger barks but you won't hate him.   Nobody could. He's so sweet, you'll want to eat him, and he's white and he's so brave though he's no bigger than *this*.'   She measured off a length with her hands.

As they walked along, Annabella noticed how

sweet and fresh the air was. There was a hint of rain. She could hear water trickling somewhere. They came to a stream which ran among stones and over some of them in a little cascade. They crossed a small stone bridge. . . .

It was the first of October.

CHAPTER 2

A NEW RECRUIT

I

When they arrived at the foot of the long street, which ran sharply uphill, Annabella's feelings of dismay returned. She had been brought up on a fruit farm—bananas and pineapples—in the Transvaal, and she was used to plenty of space. And even her aunt's house in London, which she had just left, was one of a row which ran along one side of the street only. But her two new friends urged her onwards and upwards.

'Where's the coal?' said Annabella, a new horror crossing her mind; she stopped to look round her.

'The what?' said Theo.

'The coal. Don't you have coal here? I thought you did.'

'Oh, yes, of course we do,' said Theo proudly. 'You are now standing near the edge of the biggest coal-basin in the world—made of the very best coal in the world. But the edge is a couple of miles from here, higher up the valley.'

'I don't understand,' said Annabella.

'Look,' said Theo. 'Imagine you're standing on the edge of a huge pudding-basin.'

'All right,' said Annabella, looking down between her toes, and thinking how hard it would be to perch on the edge of anything so slippery, unless you were a bird.

'Well, now imagine that it's a *black* basin, can you?'

Annabella instantly turned the basin from white to black.

'That's how the coal-basin is—but it doesn't begin here. There are outcrops of coal a couple of miles away, where they do open-cast mining. But the best coal is got out of the deep mines. You can understand that the farther you go from the edge of the basin towards the centre of it, the deeper down is the coal.'

'Yes. I see.'

'You know what coal really is, of course?' said Theo, as if no-one could be so ignorant as not to know an important thing like that.

Annabella said vaguely:

'I have an idea it has something to do with old wood—tree trunks and things—that have been buried underground and rotted. But I'm not quite sure how they become coal, like the coal we use.'

'Oh, that's easy,' said Theo cheerfully. 'Coal is really a fossil.'

' A what ? ' said Annabella.

' Don't bother her *now*, Theo,' protested Julie.
' Let's have tea first. She'll hear plenty about coal
later, whether she wants to or not.'

' All right,' said Theo, obviously disappointed
at not being allowed to finish her talk. ' I was only
going to tell her that it takes millions of years to
make coal. Once you grasp *that*, the rest's easy.
But if you're not interested——'

' Oh, but I am ! ' Annabella said eagerly, though
she was longing for her tea. ' I am really ! '

' We'll take you down a pit some time, if you
like,' Theo said. ' You go down in a cage——'

' In a cage ? '

' A cage,' Theo said, ' is a kind of lift that
whizzes down from the surface to the pit bottom.
You go down very fast : it brings your heart right
up into your mouth. You'll like that ! '

' Oh, I'll love it ! ' Annabella said fervently.

They went uphill at a good pace. Annabella
noticed that the centre of the street was ' unmade ',
that is, it had been left unsurfaced, and there were
deep ruts in it and stones sticking out where the
rainwater from the mountain ran down in little
streams.

Soon they were outside the door of the Williams'
house, which was number fifty-two. The figures
were on the door in brass, the door was green

painted, and it had a bright brass knocker and letter box. But they did not need to knock; Theo put her hand through the letter box and pulled a string, and the door opened.

2

There was a glorious smell of cakes cooking. Annabella realised how hungry she was, for she had eaten nothing, except a few sandwiches in the train, since breakfast.

Mrs. Williams came out of the kitchen to meet them. She was short and plump and smiling. Her sleeves were rolled up and her hands were covered with dough, and some of the flour had got into her hair. Her hair was brushed back and done up on top of her head in a round bun, but a few wisps escaped and she brushed them back. She gave Annabella a hearty kiss.

' So this is my cousin Meg's little niece from the Transvaal. And not so little either ! Come along,' she said, ' and welcome to Treglo ! ' She turned to her own two girls. ' Daddy isn't in yet. But you can make the tea ; he won't be more than a minute now that school's out.'

Julie went into the back kitchen to make the tea, and Annabella took off her hat and coat.

The kitchen was warm, with a big stove, and the table was laid.

At that moment a little dog ran along the linoleum-covered passage to the front door, and sounds of the door opening and shutting were heard, then footsteps.

' Here's Daddy ! ' said Theo. She turned to Annabella. ' I do hope you'll really like Roger.'

' Roger ? ' said Annabella.

' Yes. You said you disliked barking dogs. Well, Roger barks—most terriers do—he's a sort of a terrier—but only when Daddy comes home. We rather like it, you know.'

' Of course I'll like him,' said Annabella. ' But will he like me ? Maybe he hates strangers.'

' Daddy's so funny ! ' Theo said with a giggle. ' We have a string on the door, but *he* always uses his key. He says it's more dignified. You know he's a headmaster, don't you ? '

At that moment Mr. Williams entered.

He was not very tall, but he was really taller than he looked at first, because he stooped. He had grey hair and a grey moustache, and he wore a grey suit, and he usually had one hand—his right hand—in his pocket.

As he came into the kitchen, through a door which had panes of coloured glass in it, Roger danced round him, trying to attract his attention; Annabella wasn't surprised, for she thought she

had never seen a kinder-looking man in her life—
anyway, not a kinder-looking schoolmaster.

He kissed his daughter Theo, and his daughter
Julie, and his wife who came in from the back
kitchen to greet him, and then he shook hands with
Annabella.

' My ! ' he said. ' What a good smell ! But why
aren't you all sitting down at the table stuffing ? '

He sat down himself at one end, and Roger,
quiet now except for a few rumbles of satisfaction,
lay down under the table and put his white muzzle
on his master's shiny black boot, and stared up
at him.

' Who's going to pour out ? ' asked Mr. Williams.

Mrs. Williams came in carrying a plate piled
high with cakes.

' These are our local speciality, my dear,' she
said to Annabella. ' Eat them while they're hot.
And don't be afraid, they'll do you no harm, and
they're not so good next day.'

Annabella needed no second invitation. She
thought she had never tasted anything so good as
those hot cakes. And the pile disappeared as
' hot cakes ' proverbially do ; for Theo and Julie
kept pace with Annabella, and Mr. Williams had
a few, and even Roger was given one, though
Mr. Williams assured him it was for the last time,
as they were not good for him like hard biscuits.

He shook hands with Annabella

'But,' said Mr. Williams, looking round with a smile, 'if we all ate only what was good for us, we might still be living on roots and fruits, like Boadicea and her daughters—eh, my dear?'

'Well,' Theo said, 'roots and fruits are quite nice if they're carrots and potatoes, apples and oranges and nuts and things like that. Don't you love nuts yourself?'

'If those women had known about girdle-cakes,' said Mr. Williams, 'they might have been less—bellicose.'

'But,' argued Theo, 'that would have been a bad thing, Daddy! For they fought the Romans.'

'My dear,' Mr. Williams said, 'why do you assume that it was a *good* thing to fight the Romans?'

'I don't know,' Theo said, 'I always thought . . .' She stopped abruptly.

'My elder daughter,' said Mr. Williams, turning to Annabella, 'is a great one for an argument, as you'll find out, I don't doubt. Are *you* argumentative?'

'I don't know,' said Annabella. 'I think I may be—Aunt Meg often says to me " Don't argue! " but that's when I'm simply explaining to her what's right.'

Mr. Williams glanced at Mrs. Williams and smiled.

'Another recruit,' he said, 'to our village

Debating Society, I hope. And there you are, Theo: how about this as your next subject for debate ?— " Were the Britons right to resist the Romans ? " '

' Good idea,' said Theo. ' Will you speak, Annabella ? I'll take the affirmative, and you can take the negative.'

' But,' said Annabella, ' I don't know anything about the Romans. And I don't know how to— to debate.'

' Goodness ! ' said Theo in surprise. ' Never mind : you come with me tomorrow evening—and see how it's done. Daddy can coach you on the Romans.'

' Oh,' said Mr. Williams, ' you'll have to give me time to swot up the subject myself first ! '

' Daddy ! ' said Theo reproachfully, ' you know *all* about the Romans—you know you do ! '

Mr. Williams laughed.

' We have our speakers for tomorrow evening,' said Theo to Annabella, ' so there's plenty of time for you to work up your side in the debate. We only meet once every six weeks.'

3

During the evening, Daisy called.

Annabella, as it happened, opened the door.

' How is Johnnie settling down ? ' she asked anxiously.

Daisy was not of the worrying kind.

' Oh, Johnnie's all right,' she said airily.

' I meant,' said Annabella, ' how's he getting on with that other boy—Wilf, I think he was called.'

' Oh, Wilf's all right,' said Daisy.

' He seemed a bit—bellicose—to me,' said Annabella, trying out a new word.

' They were getting on fine when I left just now,' said Daisy. ' Wilf was showing Johnnie his stamp collection, and Johnnie was taking it all in. In fact, that's why Johnnie wouldn't come with me— he was so interested.'

' Good ! ' said Annabella. ' I hope it 'll last. Are you looking forward to tomorrow ? ' she asked as she escorted Daisy down the hall to the kitchen. Next morning they were to go to the new school.

' Oh, it 'll be all right ! ' said Daisy.

Annabella opened the kitchen door, and introduced her to the Williams family, whom she already felt to be like her real cousins.

When Daisy had gone Theo explained to her parents who she was, and that she and her brother Johnnie were staying with Wilf Stott and his family.

' And it's a pity,' said Theo finally.

' Why ? ' asked Annabella anxiously, all her dislike of Wilf Stott reviving.

'Because,' said Theo primly, 'Wilf Stott is a bad influence in the village.'

'Why do you say so ?' Annabella said, glancing at Mr. Williams to see if he agreed.

'Come, come, Theo !' Mr. Williams said, giving Roger the last of the cakes. 'There's not much wrong with Wilf—nothing that time won't cure.'

'You say that, Daddy,' retorted Theo, 'because Wilf was always one of your best pupils and got a scholarship to Melintre.' She turned eagerly to Annabella. 'Of course, Wilf *is* very clever ; you'll see his name in gold letters on the Honours Board of the school when Daddy takes you round. But —the fact that Wilf is clever makes his influence all the stronger. *And* he's good at games too, unfortunately. He plays rugger for the school, and in the summer he's captain of the second eleven. Wilf's just everything and everywhere.'

Mr. Williams, seeing that Annabella was bewildered, explained with a smile.

'What Theo means, Annabella, is that Wilf Stott won't do what *she* wants him to.'

'Oh, Daddy !' Theo said so indignantly that Roger barked. 'That's not fair ; I only ask people to do—what they *ought* to do.'

'And you are the sole judge of that, I suppose ?' said Mr. Williams. Then, seeing that Theo was looking a little downcast, he added, 'What Theo means precisely is, Wilf won't join her Debating Society. And it is a pity, for he could be an asset, because he has the makings of a good speaker.'

Mrs Williams joined in.

'I don't think it's *that* so much, dear, that Theo minds. But it's just that Wilf won't take part in anything at all that's got up in the village. The Stotts are all like that. Mrs. Stott just won't join the Women's Institute.'

'Wilf has a swelled head,' put in Julie.

'Clever people often have,' Mr. Williams said, 'when they're young. He'll grow out of it.'

'Yes, Daddy,' Theo said, 'but meanwhile he's doing so much harm. It wouldn't matter that he won't do things himself—but he prevents other people from joining——'

Mr. Williams leaned forward.

'Theo,' he said suspiciously, 'you've got some new scheme brewing. Now I hope it's not another Christmas play. You upset *my* school, and you also drag the grown-ups in. I refuse——'

'Daddy,' said Theo, 'it has nothing to do with the Christmas play. We started *that* last August. No, but I'm trying to stir up interest in the St. John.'

'St. John?' Annabella said, switching her thoughts from Boadicea and Wilf Stott, and confusing them with each other.

'Do you mean to say,' Theo said, 'you've never heard of the Venerable Order of St. John of Jerusalem ? You've heard of the Red Cross ? '

'Of course.'

'Well, St. John is like that in a way, but it goes on all the time. You learn First Aid. I am trying to form a Cadet Group of the St. John Ambulance, Treglo Division. Two Groups rather—one for boys, and one for girls.'

'Now that's a very good idea,' Mr. Williams said.

'Daddy and Mummy belong to the Adult Group,' Theo said.

'What do Cadet Groups do ? ' Annabella said.

'We meet once a week, and we have a lecture and an exercise. We train for competitions. And there will be all sorts of fun too—parties at Christmas, and picnics in the summer. And meanwhile, we're learning how to deal with an accident—by ourselves—if we should come across one.'

'A real accident ? '

'Oh, yes, on the road for instance. What would *you* do, Annabella, if you found a man lying in the middle of the road bleeding like mad from his head, and you knew he'd been knocked down by a car which had driven on without stopping ? '

'I'd run as fast as I could, of course,' Annabella said, 'for the doctor—or the police.'

' And leave the man in the middle of the road to be run over by the next car ? ' said Mr. Williams.

' Or leave him there to bleed to death ? ' said Theo.

' Well, what *could* I do ? ' said Annabella, feeling herself attacked on all sides.

' Join the St. John and become a Cadet,' said Mr. Williams, ' and find out.'

' Will you, Annabella ? ' Theo cried with sparkling eyes.

' Of course I will ! ' said Annabella.

Everybody cheered, and Roger barked.

CHAPTER 3

SOME SMALL HAPPENINGS

I

But before Annabella had time even to join the Cadet Ambulance Division and get some training in First Aid, several things happened to help her to make up her mind.

The first thing was, she saw what was the narrowest escape she had ever seen. There was nearly a very bad accident at Treglo cross-roads : a very dangerous corner.

Now I should like to explain again, in more detail, what the village of Treglo looked like ; then you can imagine exactly what happened.

As I said before, there was a main road, not very wide, with high hedges. On a corner there was a public house with a wide space in front of it where cars could be parked, and in this space a telephone call box. Coming on to the main road cars had to be very careful. Annabella saw a car, with Mr. Stott in it, come out on its wrong side and nearly collide with a motor bike going too fast. She thought 'whatever should I have done if they *had* collided ? '

When you turned right here off the main road, you went straight towards the village. You would go down a steep hill where the road dipped under the railway bridge. The road was very stony and in wet weather it ran with water in several streams where the rain had made deep ruts in the surface.

The railway line above ran on up the valley towards the big coal-field, or down the valley to the docks and the sea. Just beyond the bridge was the station for Treglo ; it was really little more than a railway halt, for it had no shelter or ticket office, there was just a platform on either side of the lines, and it could be very cold and windy at times. There was a bridge crossing the lines, and a level crossing which most people used rather than climb the steps of the bridge, because there wasn't much danger of being knocked down by a train. The passenger trains were very few each day and everybody in the village knew exactly when they were. The only danger was from the goods trains which came down the valley carrying coal, or going up again empty. But the goods trains moved so slowly and made so much noise that you could hardly fail to see or hear them coming, and in fact many people used to cross the lines when a goods train was approaching. The station porter (whom everybody knew) did not like this, but he never said anything to the grown-ups. He used to shout at the children if they ran across the lines in front of a train, but they took no notice.

From the station you could see the ring of hills that surrounded Treglo. There was one on the other side of the main road, about which she was to know more later. On the top of some of the more distant hills there were coal-tips—all the rubbish from the mines tipped out there and forming a huge pyramid.

2

But to come back to the road.

When you went under the railway bridge the road began to rise again, quite steeply, and in a minute you were in the village.

There was only one shop and no petrol pumps ; in fact, people seldom came to Treglo unless they lived there. They did most of their shopping in the town and bought petrol from a garage on the main road. Most of the people who lived in Treglo left it at least once a day for some reason or other.

The road, as I said before, climbed sharply upwards between two rows of houses.

The houses were strongly built of stone—a sort of ironstone found in the neighbourhood. They looked rather dark and small from the outside but inside they were snug and comfortable.

On the left as you walked up, the houses were numbered with even numbers, and on the right-hand side with the odd numbers. But everybody knew where everybody lived. You would only have had to ask for Mr. Stott's house, and anybody would have directed you to number twenty-two. To get to the house of Mr. Williams, the schoolmaster, you had to climb higher to number fifty-two.

The school where Mr. Williams was headmaster was the primary school. It lay at the foot of the hill with the church and the chapel, and there was also a small village hall where they had debates and jumble sales and other things.

At the top of the road—it was the only road in Treglo, you remember—there were open fields, and all round were small farms. Sometimes in winter the cows and sheep and the horses would walk down the street and put their heads in at the kitchen doors; and sometimes they would eat the cabbages and sprouts in the gardens. In Treglo everybody was keen on gardening and they all made the most of the small space they had behind their houses. The soil was black and fertile and the weather was usually mild though rather wet, so that it was good for growing.

Some of the people had greenhouses or glass-frames, most of them home-made; they all learnt carpentry in school, and kept it up after they left. At the proper times there used to be shows—flowers and vegetables—in the village hall. Some of the people could grow huge chrysanthemums for November or for Christmas, and others were proud of their onions or leeks or tomatoes.

There was a slight rivalry between Mr. Stott and Mr. Williams, though Mr. Williams was the mildest of men. Mr. Stott had more money than most of the people in Treglo, because he was cashier for several of the big collieries, so he could buy the best seeds and plants and also the latest fertilisers, and he spent quite a lot on heating his greenhouse with electricity; but all the same Mr. Williams, whose greenhouse was heated with a small paraffin lamp, could grow better vegetables and flowers, and he nearly always used to win the first prize for his chrysanthemums, and every year he had the most glorious show of geraniums.

This annoyed the Stotts; they seemed to think it wasn't quite fair. Mr. Stott used to try to find out what Mr. Williams did, but Mr. Williams only smiled.

3

Well, one afternoon at the end of October—it was a Saturday—Annabella was in the house all alone. Theo and Julie and Mrs. Williams had gone into town to do some shopping, and Mr. Williams had gone to a football match. Annabella was sitting by the kitchen fire reading a book.

It was very cosy in the small kitchen ; the fire was bright, everything shone as always—Mrs. Williams was a great one for polish and ' elbow grease ', as she called it—and there was no sound indoors except the ticking of the clock on the mantelpicce. Even Roger was quiet ; he had accepted Annabella as one of the family, and he lay on the black rug with his white muzzle across one of her feet. He was grand company ; if she moved, however slightly, he would show he was not really asleep by pricking his ears or by opening one of his golden eyes, which could hardly be seen through his untidy fringe of hair. He looked rather grubby, for being a white dog he could not help getting dirty in wet weather, but it was what Mrs. Williams called ' clean dirt ' (though she didn't say this when the girls brought mud in on their boots ' all over my clean floor '). It was Roger's bath night on Saturday, so that on Sundays he was like ' driven snow ', though not for very long, for he dearly loved to go up to the field at the top of the road and burrow in holes in the hedges.

Suddenly there came a tap on the kitchen door. Roger jumped up, barking.

' Quiet, Roger ! ' said Annabella. She was glad

to have him, all the same. She thought it might be a tramp or a gypsy, and it was a good thing that they shouldn't know she was here alone.

She went to the door.

Outside stood a man in a mackintosh and a corduroy cap. In his arms he held a lamb.

' Come in ! ' said Annabella politely.

The man—he was young—looked down at his heavy boots which were caked with mud, and said :

' I don't know if I should, miss. Is the Boss in ? '

' You mean Mr. Williams ? '

' Yes.'

' No, I'm afraid he's not,' said Annabella. She said it rather reluctantly, because she wasn't sure what he wanted, and she thought perhaps if she said ' the Boss ' was out, the young man might turn out to be a robber and take something. The young man said :

' My name is Tom Faggott.' He grinned. ' I come from the farm up above. In fact, my Old Man—my father—and the Boss are great pals.'

' Oh, yes,' said Annabella, relieved. She had heard Mr. Williams speak of the Faggots. She noticed that Roger was sniffing round Tom's boots in a friendly manner, though of course it might have been just the smell of mud and manure that he was enjoying : dogs like smells that humans don't much care for !

Tom stooped to pat Roger's head. The lamb he was holding on his left arm gave a frightened bleat. Roger yapped.

' Poor thing ! ' said Annabella, meaning of course the lamb.

' Yes, miss,' said Tom. He stepped inside.

' My name,' she said, ' is Annabella.'

' Oh, yes, miss,' said Tom. ' We've all heard of you.' He looked at her with some interest, and Annabella wondered *what* he had heard.

The lamb gave another bleat. Annabella noticed that one of its front legs was hanging limply down.

' You see, miss—Annabella,' said Tom, placing a big red hand on the lamb's curly head, ' this is a late-born one. It's not a good time of year to be born, miss, I can assure you, especially in the open.'

' I should think not ! ' said Annabella.

' Well, the mother just dropped him—and he went wandering about and fell down a hole. And I think he's broken his left leg. My dad says the only thing to do is to destroy him——'

' Oh ! ' said Annabella, shocked.

' Because he can't look after himself. But I said, " I'll just take him down to the Boss. *He* may be able to do something." You see, the Boss is a big man in the St. John, and bones are bones whether human or animal. And I thought perhaps the Boss—Mr. Williams—could put a splint on the little chap's leg ; at this age they heal very quickly. Then he could get about all right and nibble his grass and fodder.'

' Oh, I do wish Mr. Williams were here ! ' said Annabella. ' I'm sure he could save it ! But I don't think he'll be back till after dark. He's gone to a football match. Could you wait ? '

' Sorry, miss,' said Tom, ' I'm afraid I can't do that. You see, there's the milking as well as everything else. The little chap will have to go down the drain.'

' What ? '

' Down the drain, a tap on the head,' said Tom, making an expressive gesture. ' Don't worry ; he won't feel it.'

Annabella looked at the lamb. Its eyes seemed to be fixed on her as if pleading with her to save it. She said :

' Isn't there anyone else who could do it ? '

' I've tried the doctor,' said Tom, ' but he's out. And I haven't time to go to the vet. He wouldn't do it anyway.'

' If I found some splints and bandages, do you think you could hold it while I have a shot ? '

' Would you ? '

' Mind you, I don't know anything about it. I wish I did.   But I'll try.'

' Good ! '

Annabella went to the drawer where, she knew, Theo kept her bandages. She could not find any splints but she got two pieces of wood from the coalhouse. Tom held the lamb, which didn't seem to feel anything while Annabella placed the pieces of wood on each side of the limp little leg and wound the bandage round and round.

She did wish she knew some real First Aid.

At last Tom went off carrying the lamb. Annabella said :

' Now promise me you won't destroy him, or let anybody else, without coming here first ? '

' I won't,' said Tom cheerfully. ' I expect he'll be skipping about with the others in no time ; thank you very much, miss. Any charge ? '

' Of course not.'

' I'll bring you some cream tomorrow.'

4

When the others came in and Annabella told the story, Theo remarked :

' We don't use splints any more. They're out of date.'

'Never mind,' said Mr. Williams. 'I don't suppose the lamb cared very much if he was done according to the book or not. And you know, Theo, she couldn't have fastened a lamb's leg together according to the latest book as if he were human.'

Theo giggled.

'Oh, but,' said Annabella, 'I do wish I really knew the proper way.'

That was the first strange event. The second was even more important. It occurred less than a week later, on the fifth of November. This was always a great day in Treglo, because they had a big Guy Fawkes celebration.

5

They began preparing long before the day.

Little boys went from house to house wheeling home-made barrows, mostly soap-boxes on old wheels, with a Guy, made of old clothes stuffed with straw, lolling in the box. Annabella had never seen this before—they didn't celebrate Guy Fawkes Day where she came from—and she thought the stuffed Guy looked rather horrible. But when she said this to the other children, they only laughed; they were used to it, and many of them didn't know what the Guy meant, or why they celebrated November the Fifth at all. They just knew it was fun and there were fireworks.

The girls bought some fireworks, including Catherine Wheels and rockets and Roman Candles. Mr. Williams explained to them one evening after supper what all these things meant, for it turned out that even Theo didn't quite know why the wheels were called 'Catherine', though she wouldn't admit it for a long time. Mr. Williams explained that St. Catherine suffered martyrdom on a wheel and that was how the firework got its name.

'Stupid business altogether,' said Mr. Williams; 'a lot of noise which terrifies the cats and dogs. By the way, my dear,' he said to Mrs. Williams, 'let's be sure Roger is safely locked up in the house that night.'

'Oh, yes, Daddy,' said Julie. 'There was a letter in the paper asking us to be sure to do that. I think it was from the secretary of the R.S.P.C.A.'

'What's that?' said Annabella.

'The Royal Society for the Prevention of Cruelty to Animals,' said Theo. 'They always remind us in school too on the morning of November the Fifth.'

'They ought to do it sooner,' said Mr. Williams. 'I do. The youngsters nowadays begin letting off fireworks long before the Fifth.' He got up. 'Well, let's hope it rains in torrents on the night.'

' Oh, Daddy ! ' said Theo reproachfully. ' How can you wish anything so horrid. You know the village always has a huge bonfire ! '

' Yes, dear, *I* know,' said Mr. Williams with a funny little smile. ' And what is the bonfire for ? '

' To get rid of a lot of old rubbish, I should think,' said Mrs. Williams. ' I know I gave the boys three barrowloads of old papers and cardboard boxes for the bonfire. And jolly glad I was to get rid of them ! I could never have burnt them here.'

' Yes, but what do they put on top of the bonfire ? ' said Mr. Williams.

' The Guy ! ' said Theo and Julie together.

' Exactly,' said Mr. Williams. He took down Roger's lead from a hook on the dresser. ' Come on, boy ! Let's go for a walk. You'll be all right with Father ! '

They left, Roger leaping round and round his master.

' I didn't know Roger was ever afraid of anything,' said Annabella.

' He isn't,' said Theo proudly. ' But *all* dogs are afraid of fireworks. I suppose they think it's a pistol-shot.'

' How would they know about pistols ? ' said Annabella.

' Oh, well,' said Theo, ' perhaps it's just instinct. Anyway I know when Roger hears a crack, he creeps away to his basket under the dresser, with his tail between his legs. He looks so funny because he has such a fat stumpy little tail!' She laughed.

Mr. Williams looked into the kitchen again. He said to his wife:

'My dear, have we got everything necessary against burns? You know what always happens. And in the case of burns, Annabella, it is very important to act quickly. *First* Aid is everything. Do you know how to treat burns?'

'I'm afraid I don't,' said Annabella, 'but I have put my name down for the class.'

'Good! And when does the class start?'

'November the ninth,' said Theo.

Mr. Williams laughed.

6

On the night of the Fifth it was raining. It had been raining most of the week, but the celebrations were to be held; the huge heap of paper and rags in the field at the top of the hill had been soaked with paraffin—'Such a waste!' said Mrs. Williams, 'and dangerous too.' She and Mr. Williams left the house early; they wore their St. John uniforms and took with them their First Aid kit.

'Now, girls,' said Mrs. Williams, 'put on your mackintoshes and rubber boots, and mind you don't go too near the fire.'

'Be sure to keep on the windward side,' remarked Mr. Williams, 'so that the flames don't blow towards you.'

'I would rather they stayed at home and looked after Roger,' said Mrs. Williams with a glance at her husband. But he said:

'You can't expect them to do *that*, my dear. Did *you* stay in when you were their age?'

They smiled at each other, and left.

Julie said:

'I think *I'll* stay with Roger.'

Roger, having heard one or two bangs outside, had already crept into his basket under the dresser.

By the time Theo and Annabella had walked up the road and reached the field the bonfire was blazing merrily. Crowds were there, grown-ups as well as children, and they were dancing all round. They reminded Annabella of a picture in one of the books at home—*Robinson Crusoe*. The picture showed some black savages dancing round a fire, and as they were cannibals the picture had always rather frightened her. She thought the people round this bonfire looked rather like the savages, except that of course they—the people—

were fully dressed and had white faces which were lit up by the flames.

The rain had ceased, and a wind had sprung up, blowing away the clouds. The stars were out. The field was sodden and muddy, and it was easy to slip and fall. It was, Annabella knew, one of Tom Faggot's father's fields. She met Tom wandering on the outskirts of the crowd. He looked unhappy.

' How's the lamb ? ' she asked him.

He seemed at first to have forgotten—evidently his mind was full of other things—then he said :

' Oh, the lamb ! Oh, he's all right. Running about with the others, and even playing " King of the Castle " with them.'

' Good ! You look worried.'

' I *am* worried,' said Tom. ' My father always lends this field for Guy Fawkes night, and it's a terrible mess afterwards—no good for anything. The grass is all burnt and trampled on, and bits of fireworks are everywhere. Silly affair, I call it.'

' That's what Mr. Williams says,' said Annabella.

' He's a wise one, the Boss,' said Tom. ' And no spoil-sport either. I bet he's here tonight ? '

' He is,' said Annabella, ' and Mrs. Williams. They've come to do First Aid on anyone who gets injured.'

' *I'm* worried about our haystacks and our thatched roof,' said Tom.

' But surely the farm's a long way off ? ' said Annabella.

' Yes, but the wind has sprung up and the sparks are flying. Oh, I'm not really afraid of the sparks. Dad wouldn't let them have the field if there were any danger from sparks. But who knows whether one of the lads—or lasses—may not let off a squib in the farmyard ? '

' The squibs soon go out,' said Annabella.

' I know—especially as the ground's still wet, thank goodness. But—the noise scares the animals. The horses go nearly crazy, and as for the cows—you'll all have sour milk to-morrow in Treglo, I'm thinking.' He laughed and tramped off.

Soon afterwards Annabella heard a shriek.

Near her were a group of small boys; the smallest of them had a Catherine Wheel on a pin which he was holding in his hand, and another boy had set the end alight. The Catherine Wheel started slowly, then it began to spin round faster and faster, showing all its lovely colours and throwing off showers of sparks.

The boys all ran off, and the smallest boy— his name was Joe—was left standing alone. He yelled with fear and pain, but he seemed unable to let go of the Catherine Wheel. Annabella went up to him.

'Drop it!' she said sharply, and when he did not do so she snatched it from him, threw it on to wet soil, and stamped on it. She heard a familiar voice behind her. It was Mr. Williams.

'Good girl!' he said. 'Are you hurt?'

'No, thank you—but I think this little boy is.'

Joe roared loudly.

'Now Joe,' said Mr. Williams, patting his head, 'this is where you show yourself a man.' Joe still roared. Mr. Williams said to Annabella, 'Find my wife, will you? She has the First Aid box. This is the sixteenth burn we have treated tonight. She also has some lollipops—one for Joe, if he's brave.'

Joe stopped crying, and Annabella ran off.

She held a torch while they dressed Joe's burn.

'The essential thing about treating a burn,' said Mr. Williams, 'is to exclude air at the beginning. But don't let anybody mess it up with grease or oil or butter or cooking fat.'

They tied Joe's hand up in a neat bandage, and Mrs. Williams took him to his mother.

'I wish I had known what to do,' said Annabella the next day. 'I felt so stupid just looking on holding a torch.'

'Drop it!'

'You soon will,' said Theo. 'Remember, we begin on Monday.'

'It can't be too soon for me,' said Annabella, collecting her hat, coat and books to go to school.

7

On Sunday mornings Mr. Williams had his breakfast in bed, and the girls got breakfast downstairs. Mrs. Williams didn't want to stay in bed, but they all insisted that she must rest, she worked so hard all the rest of the week.

Annabella liked to help. On the Sunday after Guy Fawkes night she carried up the breakfast tray, which had on it Mrs. Williams's own large pot of tea. Annabella placed the tray on the edge of the bed, when to her dismay she saw it beginning to slide, and before she could stop it everything had fallen on to the floor.

This was bad enough, but nothing broke, and all might have been well except that the whole pot of tea emptied itself on to Annabella's foot !

The tea was almost boiling, and Annabella felt an agonising pain ; the teapot did not break but the cosy and lid came off, and the pot lay on its side ; the tea-leaves lay on Annabella's foot like a hot poultice, and she seemed unable to do anything except hop about the room on the other foot.

Mrs. Williams, looking on from the bed, said : ' What's the matter, dear ? '

' My foot ! ' gasped Annabella, hardly able to speak for the pain.

Mrs. Williams jumped out of bed, and ran Annabella into the bathroom ; she stripped off Annabella's white sock, and turned on the bath-tap. As soon as the water covered the bottom of the bath, she made Annabella sit on the edge of the bath and plunge her foot—it was the right foot— under the water, while she called out to the others to come upstairs.

Now that her foot was under water, Annabella could feel no pain. Looking down, she could see a large patch of red skin on the inner side, and she remembered the awful blister she had had when she had once dropped hot sealing-wax on her hand. She wondered if the red skin on her foot could become a blister, and if blisters could be so large. ' Perhaps,' she thought, ' all the skin will come off. . . .'

Mrs. Williams came back.

She got Annabella to bring her foot out of the water ; then she very gently laid on the red skin a piece of gauze soaked in some kind of yellow ointment. Then she laid on that some

Annabella plunged her foot into the bath

cotton wool, and then she bandaged it. The foot was now enormous, and Annabella could not put on her shoe. Theo, acting on her mother's instructions, brought an old bedroom slipper of her father's, and this they put on the injured foot. Mrs. Williams would not let Annabella go to church that morning : she made her lie on her bed or on the sofa in the kitchen.

'How long shall I have to stay in for ?' said Annabella. 'I don't want to miss anything.'

'You won't,' said Mr. Williams. 'You'll be in school the day after tomorrow. I'll ring them up and tell them you've taken to playing football with our best teapot.'

The doctor came in during the morning and said that Annabella's foot could be left just as it was ; Mrs. Williams had saved it from any serious damage by her prompt action. It was an elderly doctor, the older of the two partners, and he liked to poke fun at people :

'I didn't know you First Aiders were so good,' he said to Mrs. Williams ; and to Annabella, 'Young lady, I'm afraid there'll be nothing to stop you from going to school the day after tomorrow.'

'I *like* school,' said Annabella.

8

We may as well say at once that Annabella did not have to stay home from school for more than one day, nor did she have to miss anything. Her foot was left in its bandage for a week and she was asked many questions about it as she hobbled about in Mr. Williams's bedroom slipper ; but the skin didn't come off, and when the gauze dressing was finally removed, there was no sign of the burn except a certain redness ; and soon Annabella could feel nothing there except a slight irritation.

Before long she forgot all about it. But she did not forget the kindness and skill of Mrs. Williams, and how she herself in the same circumstances wouldn't have known what to do.

CHAPTER 4

A CLASH OF WILLS

I

By the time that Annabella had been staying in Treglo for a month or so, she knew everybody and everybody knew her.

She had settled down happily at Melintre School and she enjoyed the daily bus ride to and from the school along the country lanes with the other contingent from Treglo. The lanes were so narrow that often the hedges swept the windows of the bus, and the branches of overhanging trees struck the roof. She had her dinner in school, and this was fun too.

Theo and Julie also came in the bus, and Daisy, but not Johnnie who always went by train with Wilf Stott. Annabella saw very little of her old friends now: Daisy was in the form below hers, and Johnnie was in the form above. Also, Annabella's time was very much taken up; she had joined everything there was to join, not only in the school but in the village.

One evening after school, thinking she was getting out of touch with Johnnie and Daisy, she went down to the Stotts to pay them a call. She was invited to walk upstairs to Wilf's 'den'.

Here she found Wilf and Johnnie absorbed in a game of chess, which Wilf was teaching Johnnie. They did not look up for a moment, and when Johnnie did look up and saw who it was, he frowned.

'Sorry if I'm intruding,' Annabella said, drawing herself up to her full height.

'Oh, it's all right,' Johnnie said. 'Only I was just beginning to grasp something and now I've lost it.' She noticed that he had a book about chess open on the table beside him, and that he looked very worried, not as if he were enjoying a game.

Annabella said:

'Isn't it rather a strain after a day's work? I prefer Snakes and Ladders myself.'

She thought she overheard Wilf remark:

'You *would*,' but as it was not said directly to her but was muttered to himself over the chess board, she decided not to hear. She said:

'I just came to ask you, Johnnie, if you and Daisy are coming to the Junior Debating Society meeting tomorrow night in the hall.'

She noticed that Johnnie cast an inquiring glance at Wilf before he answered:

'Daisy can go if she likes. But I'm afraid I can't. I'm busy.'

'Sorry if I'm intruding'

' I'm one of the speakers,' she said, not meaning to sound self-important, but because she thought Johnnie would come to support her if he knew.

Wilf plunged a hand through his hair as if he were trying to concentrate, and this time she distinctly heard him mutter :

' You *would* be ! '

Annabella came farther into the den :

' Wilf Stott,' she said firmly, ' I know you can't help being rude—but can't you refrain to a visitor in your own house ? I came here to see Johnnie, not you ; he and Daisy are old friends of mine. Will you please let him speak for himself ? Johnnie, will you come tomorrow night, or not ? '

There was a most uncomfortable silence. Then Johnnie said :

' What's the debate about ? '

Annabella eagerly seized the chance to explain :

' The question before the House,' she said, ' will be " That it was a mistake for the Britons to resist the Romans ", and Theo is taking the affirmative—that it *was* a mistake—and I am taking the negative—that they were right to fight. Mr. Williams has coached us both, and I think it will be fun.'

Johnnie looked undecided. Then he said :

' Will you come, Wilf ? '

Wilf said :

'What? Come and listen to a couple of school-girls saying what they don't believe about things of which they know nothing? No fear!'

Annabella glanced at Johnnie and saw him laugh as Wilf glanced at him.

'All right,' Annabella said haughtily. 'Please yourselves!' And she flounced out of the room and shut the door, not very gently; over the noise it made she heard Johnnie say:

'Annabella! I'm sorry!'

Wilf let out a whistle of relief and said:

'*Now* we can get on. You must concentrate, old chap.'

At the front door, she met Daisy coming in.

'What on earth has happened to Johnnie?' Annabella said.

Daisy looked alarmed.

'What do you mean?'

'I mean, he seems unable to do anything without first getting Wilf's approval.'

'Oh, that's nothing,' Daisy said, looking relieved. 'Boys will be boys, you know. Did you want anything specially?'

'No. Oh, well, I came to ask him—and you, of course—if you are coming to the Debating Society tomorrow night. I suppose you won't want to either.'

'Won't I?' Daisy said. 'I wouldn't miss

coming for anything.   You *have* got a nerve,
Annabella, standing up in front of everybody and
making an ass of yourself.   But you were always
brave.'

' I came to ask you—and him—something else,'
Annabella said.   ' But evidently this isn't the
moment.   I'll try another time.'

' Yes, do,' said Daisy, obviously glad to see her
go away.

2

What Annabella had wanted to ask them was if
they would join the Cadet Groups of the St. John
Ambulance Division.   She herself had joined and
was enjoying it immensely.

There were two groups of Cadets : one for boys
and one for girls.   The grown-ups had classes too,
and it was a Mrs. Sound, who went to the Adult
First Aid Class, who taught the girl Cadets, and a
Mr. Herring, who attended the same grown-ups'
class, who trained the boys.   Mrs. Sound and Mr.
Herring lived in the one street of Treglo.   Mrs.
Sound was a nurse, and Mr. Herring was a miner.
After they had had their lecture, the girls and
boys practised what they had learnt—bandaging,
how to look for injuries, and what to do before the
doctor comes.   They wore uniforms : for the
grown-ups there were very smart uniforms in

black and silver, and for the girl Cadets there were
grey cotton dresses with black berets, or white
fly-away handkerchief head-dresses.

At the end of the course, if they passed their
examination, they would be given certificates.
They would also receive badges for proficiency
and length of service. Then when they were old
enough they could join the Adult Classes. Annabella was present for the first time in her life at
a Presentation of Awards, and she saw and heard
the Cadets making the fine promises of the Cadet
Code of Chivalry :

> To serve God.
> To be loyal to the Queen and to my Officers.
> To observe the mottoes of the Order :
>   ' Pro Fide '—For the Faith
>   ' Pro Utilitate Hominum '—For the Service
>   of Mankind.
> To be thorough in work and play.
> To be truthful and just in all things.
> To be cheerful and prompt in all I do.
> To help the suffering and the needy.
> To be kind to all animals.

She also watched the grown-ups doing an exercise,
in which one of the class, Bob Brook, pretended to
be the injured man : he lay on the ground groaning

and was supposed to have broken a leg, and to be
bleeding from a cut artery in his head. The
trickle of glycerine and cochineal looked very real
and made her feel rather queer. She saw the team
under their captain, who was Mr. Williams, run
forward with a stretcher, ask the 'injured' man—
who was supposed to be conscious—a number of
questions, and deal first with the haemorrhage,
and then with the fractured leg. Mr. Herring,
their instructor, then criticised their efforts, and
this for the Cadets was very amusing, for serious
mistakes were being made by their parents and
teachers who were supposed always to do everything right.

As Mr. Herring went off, leaving the grown-ups
to discuss the work, Theo who was sitting beside
Annabella, ran after him.

' Mr. Herring ! ' she said.

He turned.

' My friend Annabella wants to go down a pit,'
she said. ' She comes from South Africa and she
knows very little about coal, though she knows
lots about pineapples. Do you think it can be
managed ? '

' I daresay,' Mr. Herring said, after a moment's
silence. ' But don't they arrange such things in
your school ? '

' Yes,' said Theo, ' but I thought it would be

nicer for Annabella if we took her in a small party led by an—an *expert*—like yourself—and then she could see better and ask questions. Annabella's always asking questions,' she said, looking round and beckoning Annabella to come nearer.

'I'll see what I can do,' Mr. Herring said. 'I rather like answering questions as it happens, if they're not silly ones.' When Annabella came up he said, 'You made a very good speech the other night; if I'd had a vote, I'd have voted for you and the Romans—though I'm an ancient Briton myself by descent.'

'I've often wondered,' said Mr. Williams, coming up, 'where we'd be now if it hadn't been for the Romans?'

The two girls left them debating the question all over again.

3

Annabella managed to catch Johnnie alone one day in the playground, and she asked him to join the St. John. He looked at her and then at the ground.

'My time's all taken up,' he said, 'with more important things.'

'Nothing can be more important,' said Annabella, 'than First Aid. Think of the lives that were saved by it in air raids during the war!'

She had heard of this not only from Theo, but also from her aunt and uncle in London.

' Well, there's no war on now! ' Johnnie said.

' But there are all kinds of accidents,' Annabella said. She thought she saw his glance wandering, and she was not surprised to find Wilf Stott coming towards them.

' Sorry, I've no time,' Johnnie said and turned away.

' *Don't* tell me you're still on about the St. John business ! ' Wilf said as he joined them. ' Annabella, you really are a nuisance ! You're getting as bad as—if not worse than—Theo Williams. Boys haven't time for an amateurish racket like First Aid. My father says it does more harm than good—and that he'd be terrified if he fell into the hands of one of you First Aiders ! And so would I.'

' Oh ! ' retorted Annabella, ' I suppose you and your father would rather be left to bleed to death in the middle of the road because you didn't know where to find each other's pressure-points ! '

' Come on, Johnnie,' Wilf said, ' you've got to change.' Wilf was using his influence to slip Johnnie into the first fifteen.

' I wish,' Annabella said, ' you'd let Johnnie make up his own mind. As for you, Johnnie, soon

you'll have no mind left to make up if you hand
what you've got on a plate to Wilf ! '

' Well, really, Annabella,' Johnnie said, ' I might
come, only . . .'

She could see that her shaft had gone home, and
she hoped that he might get tired of being ' run '
by Wilf Stott. So for the present she decided to
leave well alone.

CHAPTER 5

THE ACCIDENT

I

By the time Annabella had been in Treglo for a month, she had settled down as happily in her new school as if she had never known any other. Everywhere there was modern, much more modern than in the school in London which was now at last being improved. At Melintre there were not only large classrooms with lots of light, but also a splendid art room and a completely up-to-date laboratory. There was a fine gymnasium and playing fields, and in their Great Hall they had a permanent stage with proper lighting and an electrically worked curtain. Most of the members of the staff, masters and mistresses, believed in the value of dramatic presentations, and let the pupils act extracts from the plays and books they were reading. Annabella loved this.

Nevertheless, what she most enjoyed was getting home to tea where there was always a welcome from Mrs. Williams, and eating her lovely cakes and sometimes her home-made bread, and the apple dumplings which were as good as her Aunt Meg

had said they were. Cream came regularly on
Sundays from Mr. Faggot; and Mrs. Williams had
a sister who lived in Devonshire and who used to
send her tins of thick Devonshire cream. When
one of these arrived Mrs. Williams would make
the kind of scones which are called 'splits', and
they would be eaten cut in half and filled with
cream and honey, or cream and golden syrup.

Then they might all go out, Theo and Julie and
Annabella and sometimes Mr. and Mrs. Williams
too. There seemed to be always something on in
the village at night, and when they all set out
and went down the steep hill to the village hall or
the school or the chapel, Annabella found it the
greatest fun. It was usually raining—it rained a
great deal in Treglo—yet in the direction of the
nearest town you could often see a dull red glow
in the sky. Mr. Williams explained that this was
not a fire as Annabella at first thought, but that
the blast furnaces of the steel works were being
opened.

2

One night when there was nothing on the three
girls were sitting in the kitchen reading. They
could hear the rain beating against the window,
but inside it was warm and cosy. Mr. and Mrs.
Williams had gone to the cinema in town.

Suddenly there came a violent banging on the front door.

' What's that ? ' said Julie, who was inclined to be nervous.

' How should I know ? ' Theo said. ' Go and see ! '

' No. *You* go ! ' Julie said.

The hammering on the door started again, louder than ever. This time it did not stop.

The two sisters looked at each other, but neither got up.

' *I'll* go,' Annabella said, realising that Theo was frightened too, but did want to say so. She herself, being a stranger, had no idea of anything to be afraid of. So she jumped up and ran along the hall.

As she pulled the front door open, the wind and rain seemed to swirl in, with—of all people—Wilf Stott ! He was dripping with rain from head to foot ; his hair was in streaks over his face. He stepped in—and where he stood, several pools formed as the rain dripped off his mackintosh.

' Oh, Annabella ! ' he said. ' Can you come along ? We've had an accident. I think he's hurt —not dead or anything, of course . . . I think ! '

' Who's hurt ? ' shouted Annabella. She drew Wilf along the hall into the kitchen, where Theo and Julie looked up, astonished.

'Johnnie,' said Wilf. 'You see, we stayed on to a rugger practice and then we had tea and then as we were riding home—on my bicycle—Johnnie hasn't got one of his own——'

'Both of you?' Annabella said, 'on your bicycle?'

'Well, yes. He was standing on the step. I couldn't leave him to walk, could I?'

'And I suppose you had no lamp—you never have,' said Theo.

'I have a reflector—but I think he must have been standing in front of it or something. Anyhow, as we were turning in here off the main road —under the railway bridge—a chap on a motor-bike ran into us from behind. I think he's a bit knocked about too,' said Wilf, 'but not as badly as Johnnie. He can't move—and——' He was gasping as he told the story.

'Are you hurt?' said Julie to Wilf. Julie had a kind heart. Annabella was too angry to care about Wilf. She said:

'What have you done with Johnnie? Have you left anybody to look after him? Have you sent for the doctor?'

'I phoned his house from the call-box,' Wilf said. 'But he was out. There are several chaps standing by with Johnnie, but they don't know what to do, and Daisy's there now—but she's no

help. So I thought—as you knew First Aid . . .'
His voice trailed off.

'Come on, Theo !' said Annabella. 'Let's take
all our coats and mackintoshes—we'll need them to
cover Johnnie up with—and our bandages. And I
say, Julie, suppose you make some tea. Johnnie 'll
need it when we bring him in.'

Annabella had struggled into her outdoor clothes
and put on her rubber boots ; she and Theo set
off with Wilf down the hill which was streaming
with water, like a river or several rivulets. At the
bottom there was a pond several inches deep.

When they reached the place at the side of the
road where Johnnie had been thrown, they found
a small group of men standing round. Theo took
charge, and someone shone a torch on Johnnie,
while Theo and Annabella examined him. He
looked very pale by torch-light, but he smiled
ruefully when he saw them.

'Where's the motor-cyclist ?' said Annabella,
suddenly remembering him.

'He got up and rode away, miss,' said one of the
bystanders.

'Did you get his name ?'

'No, miss.'

'Well, you should have, and the number of his
bike too, so that if he doesn't report the accident
he'll get into trouble.' She turned back to Johnnie,

who was already being asked by Theo if he could feel any pain here or there.

' But look at his head ! ' Annabella gasped.

' Oh, that's nothing ! ' said Johnnie. ' It's my arm ! I can't move it.'

Annabella examined the place where blood was coming from Johnnie's head, and she did not like what she saw. Remembering her lessons, she made a ring-pad and adjusted it so that it encircled the gash on Johnnie's head. Then she tied it on firmly with her mackintosh belt. She did not want to waste time for she could see that the cut Johnnie thought nothing of was serious. She knew he was losing arterial blood ; she could tell this by the way it pumped out. ' And now,' she said, ' we must get him under cover quickly.'

He was already protected to some extent by the coats and mackintoshes they had spread over him. But the rain was pouring down harder than ever.

' We want a stretcher,' she said, ' and volunteers.'

' Wait,' Theo said ; ' I haven't finished his arm properly.' Theo was apt to do everything according to the book and to be rather slow. Annabella felt it was important to get Johnnie into a warm, dry bed while they waited for the doctor.

At that moment Johnnie fainted.

Two men came running up with an improvised stretcher. It was a wide plank really, but they had

She tied it on firmly with her mackintosh belt

covered it with a coat and had rolled up their caps into a pillow. They lifted Johnnie on to it.

'Where shall we take him, miss?'

Annabella looked at Theo.

'Do you think your mother would mind if we took him to your place, Theo?' she said. 'Then we can examine him more carefully.'

What she really felt was that Johnnie would be better looked after in the Williams' house; but just as she was giving the order to the men, Wilf strolled up.

'No, you don't,' he said firmly. 'Take him to *our* place—not *fifty*-two, *twenty*-two.' Wilf had recovered his self-assurance, and the men hesitated and looked at Annabella.

'Oh, all right,' she said to the men. 'Take him to twenty-two. Is Daisy there?' she said to Wilf.

'Yes. She went back to get things ready.'

'Good. I only hope she knows what to do.'

The men picked up the plank with Johnnie on it, and began the walk, down under the railway bridge and then up the steep road where they all lived. Occasionally one of them stumbled on a stone in the unmade road, and Johnnie, who had revived, gave a groan.

'Awful road this,' said one of the men.

'Yes, awful. Something ought to be done about it. My wife fell and hurt her ankle the other day.'

'Who's supposed to do it?'

'I don't know. I thought it was the County Council, but they say the tenants will have to help to pay if the road's done. And no-one will.'

They trudged on, through the pouring rain, until they reached Wilf's house. The door was already open, and Daisy stood in the doorway.

'Well, goodnight,' Wilf said to Theo and Annabella. 'Take him upstairs,' he said to the men carrying Johnnie; and to Daisy: 'Is it all ready?'

'I think so,' Daisy whispered.

'You *think* so,' said Wilf scornfully. 'Don't you *know*?'

Theo and Annabella lingered, though they realised that Wilf had no intention of asking them in. Wilf said:

'Well, thank you for your help. You'd better be getting home now—or you'll catch cold. *We* can carry on.'

'Are you sure you can manage, Daisy?' Annabella said.

'Of course she can,' Wilf said quickly. 'Go on, Daisy—go and see that everything's all right.'

Daisy ran off upstairs. Wilf shut the door. Annabella said to Theo:

'I wonder if we ought to have gone right in?'

'Well,' Theo said, 'we could hardly push Wilf over, could we?'

' I'd have liked to,' Annabella said. 'After all,
we're told the patient's safety comes first—not
other people's ideas of what's best.'

' I think I made a nice job of his arm,' Theo
said as they went on their way up the road. ' I
don't think he'd broken any other bones, do you ? '

' I'm sure the arm's all right. I wish I were as
sure that I had made a good job of my ring-pad
on his head. It certainly stopped the bleeding.
But what if it slips ? Those two would have no
idea what to do—and Johnnie might bleed to death.
I think I'll go back and hammer on the door.
After all, Wilf came and hammered on our door.'

She had turned, in spite of Theo's restraining
hand on her arm, and had reached the closed door
again, when she saw the headlights of a car ; it
swung under the bridge and up the road towards
her.

' Oh, here you are ! ' said a cheerful voice.
' Which is the house where the accident case has
been taken to ? ' It was the doctor—Dr. Hann, the
junior partner.

' This one,' Annabella said. Theo came and
joined them.

' Hullo, Theodora,' said the doctor. ' Now
what's been the trouble ? Tell me all about it—
that is, if you know anything.'

They told him, but they had scarcely begun when

the door of the Stotts' flew open. Daisy came running towards them.

' Doctor, doctor, come quickly ! ' she said, gasping. ' Johnnie's arm is hurting him terribly.'

' Oh, dear ! ' Theo said, ' and I thought I'd done it so well ! '

3

When the two girls reached home they drank the tea that Julie had made for Johnnie, and went to bed with a hot-water bottle also prepared for him. ' There was *something*,' Annabella said, ' in carrying out routine precautions.'

Next morning they were none the worse for their experience. Mrs. Williams said that as it was Saturday they had better have breakfast in bed. But Annabella was too uneasy to rest for long. She got up and dressed, and went to inquire about Johnnie.

It was a lovely morning after the rain. The sky was blue with big white clouds like pillows, and the trees and bushes were all glistening with raindrops. On a tree somewhere a robin was singing shrilly and sweetly.

Annabella knocked at the Stotts' door.

Wilf opened it.

' Hullo ! ' he said. He did not look pleased to see her.

'How is Johnnie?'

'He's all right, except for a headache.'

'I should like to see him.'

'Well, you can't,' said Wilf.

'Oh, yes, I can!' Annabella said, pushing past him and climbing the stairs. Luckily the first door she opened proved to be that of Johnnie's bedroom. He smiled as she came in.

'I don't remember a thing about it,' he said when she asked him. 'One minute I was riding on the back of Wilf's bike, and it was pouring with rain; the next minute—or so it seemed—I was in bed and the doctor was telling me I'd be quite all right. And so I am,' he said, struggling up in bed, 'except for a bit of a headache.' He grinned. 'I gather you girls had a bit of fun practising your First Aid on me last night. Wilf said——'

The bedroom door opened and Dr. Hann entered, followed by Mrs. Stott and Wilf.

The doctor talked while he took Johnnie's pulse, asking him how he felt and so on.

'And this is one of the young ladies who rendered First Aid,' he ended. 'Annabella is her name, I gather.'

'It was my friend Theo and I,' Annabella said. 'Theo did his arm, and I did his head. I'm

afraid I didn't do it very well, but it's the first
time I've ever had to cope with a *real* accident——'

' You did excellently,' said the doctor. ' In fact
you saved his life. You turned the tap off, and it
was blood, not water, that was coming out of it.'

' Oh, I was so afraid I hadn't fixed that thing
firmly enough,' Annabella said. ' I always think
ring-pads are so hard—don't you ? '

The doctor laughed.

' Yes—very. I doubt if I could have done it
so well myself. But you see, *your* training is more
recent than mine. I understand you're a member
of the St John's ? '

' Yes,' said Annabella.

' Then I expect I shall have the pleasure of
examining you one day. I wish all you youngsters
would join it.'

' I'm sure Johnnie will now, Doctor,' Annabella
said quietly. She ignored Mrs. Stott and Wilf.

Johnnie cast a quick look at Wilf. But he said :

' Of course I'll join. Maybe Wilf will too. What
do you say to the idea, Wilf ? '

' That I won't,' Wilf said, turning and walking
out. Mrs. Stott looked after him admiringly.

' He's very strong-minded,' she said. ' Just like
his father.'

' Strong-mindedness is all very well,' said Dr.
Hann, ' if it's applied in the right direction.'

'Well, you see, Doctor,' Mrs. Stott said, 'Wilfred rather looks down on the St. John. He thinks it's —amateurish. *He* wants to be a *real* doctor when he grows up.'

'A little previous experience wouldn't hurt him,' said Dr. Hann. 'I wish *I'd* had it.'

'Wilf's all right,' Johnnie muttered. 'It's just that he hates to be *told* what to do. He'll join when he feels like it. Meanwhile, Annabella,' he said rather awkwardly, 'you can count *me* in. I mean it.'

'Oh, Johnnie!' said Annabella. 'That'll be marvellous!'

'And Daisy too, of course!' Johnnie said grandly.

Annabella went away well satisfied.

4

Johnnie got better quite quickly.

His arm was in plaster and he could go to school, but of course he couldn't play rugger; the doctor had put a couple of stitches in his head on the night of the accident, so he was an object of wonder to the rest of the school, and they gathered round him at play-times and in the dinner-hour to look at the place where the stitches had been. He was almost a hero, especially as he said, quite truthfully, that he hadn't felt the stitches going in.

Annabella too came in for a share of attention, and several times she was asked to show how she had put the ring-pad on Johnnie's head.

But Wilf would have nothing to do with all this. If he happened to meet Annabella, he passed her by without a word, pretending he didn't know her or hadn't seen her; but she knew he *had*, because of the queer look on his face—a sort of sneer.

Theo said, ' He's annoyed because we were proved right.'

But Annabella said :

' The thing is to take no notice. Johnnie's way is best. I think if we leave Wilf alone, he might come along—one day.'

Mr. Williams, who was sitting by the kitchen fire reading a newspaper, overheard these remarks. He said :

' Annabella's right, you know.'

' Well,' Theo said, ' exactly how many people have to be knocked down before Wilf learns sense and proves that you and Annabella are right ? '

' You know, Wilf's a born leader,' Mr. Williams said, with a smile. ' But the trouble about born leaders is, they don't like to do anything but lead.'

'He's quite welcome to lead,' Theo said, 'so far as we're concerned, if only he'll learn how.'

'Patience!' Mr. Williams said. 'History teaches us—I think it was Queen Elizabeth the First who said that most problems were solved by time.'

'Not haemorrhages!' Annabella said.

CHAPTER 6

THE COAL-MINE

I

For some weeks things went on in much the same way; Johnnie and Daisy joined the Cadet Ambulance Classes and worked hard; Annabella and Theo worked for their certificates. Johnnie and Daisy now took the school bus with the others, but Wilf Stott caught the train. He seemed to want to avoid them, and he no longer made a friend of Johnnie.

One day Annabella said to Johnnie :

' Why don't you come and stay at Number Fifty-two ? Mr. and Mrs. Williams would be glad to have you *and* Daisy—Mrs. Williams says she can easily make room—and you must be rather uncomfortable staying with the Stotts.'

' Why should I be ? ' said Johnnie. He had an obstinate look on his face that Annabella knew well, and it suddenly struck her that he and Wilf were not unlike, at any rate in this respect.

' Well,' said Annabella, trying hard not to be tactless, ' Wilf Stott and you don't seem to be as friendly as you used to be.'

'Oh, that's all right!' said Johnnie. 'Wilf's a bit disappointed that I can't play rugger—and of course he's in a higher Form, so we don't see as much of each other. But I wouldn't think of leaving. The Stotts would be offended. I wouldn't like that; they've been very kind, *I* think—just as kind as your Williams.'

'Good,' said Annabella. 'If that's how you feel, I've no more to say.'

'Good!' retorted Johnnie. 'I know jolly well what you mean: you're mad with Wilf because he won't join the St. John. As a matter of fact if you girls would just keep quiet about it, he might. If you keep on badgering him, he certainly won't. A chap hates being badgered.'

'Then I won't say anything more,' Annabella said, her eyes flashing. 'But I think it shows a very poor spirit to stay out of a good cause because you're too stubborn to admit——'

'There you go again!' Johnnie said.

Annabella said no more; though it was very hard for her not to say all she thought. But it was hardly *her* place to say, 'Theo and I saved your life with our First Aid when Wilf didn't know what to do and would have let you die.'

Johnnie, as if he had overheard her thoughts, said:

'I know you saved my life, Annabella, when

Wilf didn't know what to do. But don't you see, that's just what makes him so mad ? You showed him up.'

'Yes,' Annabella said, '*I* see.' Inside herself she thought, 'I still think it's a poor spirit.' But she admired Johnnie for sticking up for his friend.

2

Meanwhile, Annabella learnt a great deal more about the St. John Ambulance Brigade. It was exciting to know that it was a descendant of the oldest Order of Chivalry—the Venerable Order of the Hospital of John of Jerusalem, an order of knight-monks who undertook, in the days of the Crusades, to protect pilgrims on their journeys to and from the Holy Land, and to nurse and look after the sick and suffering. That, she learnt, was why among the mottoes of the Order are two : 'Pro Fide'—For the Faith, and 'Pro Utilitate Hominum'—For the Service of Mankind. The mottoes, she learnt, are in Latin because at the time when the Order was founded, Latin, the language of the Church and of scholars, was the one language understood all over the world, whether people's native tongues might be English, French, German, Italian and so on.

She learnt that the services the Cadets could render included not only First Aid, for fortunately there aren't many accidents for which they are called on to render First Aid, but also such things as running errands and doing shopping for elderly people and those who are ill. She at once offered her services, which were gratefully accepted, to an old lady, nearly blind, who lived at the top of the hill. Johnnie helped her too. He came to tidy up this old lady's back garden; he trimmed the privet hedge and cut the small square of grass and weeded the flower-bed, and he even got some glass and wood—he was good at carpentry —and made her a small frame in which she could grow a few lettuces protected from the frost.

Annabella and he used to meet at this house sometimes on Saturday mornings when she called on old Mrs. Browning for the weekly shopping list. Johnnie would be in the back garden clipping away with his shears; Annabella was pleased, but she took good care not to say anything. Johnnie might think, if she praised him, that she was badgering him in some way. So if he happened to look up and see her, she would give a nod and say ' Hullo ! ' and go.

3

One Saturday afternoon, Annabella, with Theo, Julie, Daisy and Johnnie was returning from a walk on the mountain. It was a glorious day : cold and sunny, with no wind at all, so they had decided to climb the mountain opposite ; it was a rounded hill called a mountain because it was just over a thousand feet high. From where they lived there was a fairly gentle climb up a wide grassy path through the bracken, now quite brown, to the top. On the top there was a little mound—' The Pimple' as it was called— where Mr. Williams had told them, there had been a bonfire lit on the night of the last four Coronations: those of King Edward VII, George V, George VI and Queen Elizabeth II—' and certainly before those' he had said with a twinkle. ' Possibly in the days of William the Conqueror, but I don't remember.'

They had climbed to the top of The Pimple, which was still blackened where the bonfire had been lit for the last Coronation, and had now begun the descent. There was a lovely view from the top : they could see the coastal plain, some-what misty, with a train puffing across it, and be-yond it a silvery streak which was the sea. Johnnie was rather cross because he still could not play rugger. Theo said suddenly :

' I heard some very queer noises coming out of the Stotts' house as I went past last night : was that *you*, Johnnie ? '

' No,' said Daisy quickly. ' That was Wilf ; he's practising the bugle.'

' Oh, how awful for you ! ' Theo said. Annabella gave her a nudge. Theo said : ' Why on earth is he doing that ? '

' We don't know,' Daisy said, ' but we think— he may be thinking of joining something.'

Annabella remembered that among the things a Cadet could do was to become a bugler in a Cadet Band. She thought that the subject had better be changed before somebody added something tactless. So she said :

' It should be the greatest fun next Thursday. It is all fixed, isn't it ? '

Next Thursday, it had been arranged that a small party from Melintre School should visit a coalmine.

They had been given leave of absence from school classes on Thursday morning for the visit ; there were six boys and six girls, and the boys included Johnnie and the girls included Annabella, Daisy and Theo. Wilf had been offered a place, but had refused to come. When asked, he had said :

'I know all about the mines. Let the young "foreigners" go.'

'I'm not a foreigner,' Annabella said indignantly, when Johnnie repeated this remark.

Johnnie laughed.

'He doesn't mean *you* particularly,' he said. 'He means all three of us—because we don't live here and don't belong.'

Annabella said :

'Doesn't he make you mad sometimes, Johnnie, with his rudeness ?'

'Oh,' Johnnie said, 'you don't want to take old Wilf seriously ; he's only joking. You don't understand him a bit.'

Annabella gave Johnnie a queer look :

'How's he getting on with his bugle practice ?' she said.

Johnnie put his hands over his ears.

They both laughed.

4

The party of children met at the head of the pit ; they were accompanied by Mr. Herring, their First Aid instructor, who had once worked in the pit, and by one of the younger masters, Mr. Miller, from Melintre. He taught chemistry. He was very tall and thin with black curly hair, and he had a reputation for being very clever ; certainly he knew everything about the nature of coal, and had given several lessons before they came, on coal and its byproducts, on peat and lignite.

Before they entered the pit they were given boiler-suits to put on over their clothes, and each was given a Davy Lamp to carry. Mr. Miller explained to them how the Davy Lamp came to be invented, and Mr. Herring explained its use.

They gathered that a certain Mr., later Sir, Humphry Davy, over a hundred years ago, had invented the lamp, for the sake of the safety of miners.

' Yes,' said Mr. Herring, breaking in, ' it detects the presence of gas.'

There followed a lecture from Mr. Miller on the nature of marsh-gas or methane or fire-damp as he called it, and on white-damp and black-damp. And Mr. Herring went on to say that if the Davy Lamp went out, the miner had to drop everything and run, because it meant that there was gas about, and there might be an explosion, especially if the gas was mixed with coal-dust as well.

Mr. Miller then explained the principle of the Davy Lamp, and they were each given one ; it was a small oil-lamp covered with a cylinder of wire gauze.

' This is the old-fashioned type,' said Mr. Miller; and Mr. Herring added :

' Yes, it's old-fashioned, like many of the miners, and the best miners too, eh? But it does the job.'

' But,' said one of the boys, ' if the lamp goes out what's the good of that? You're left in the dark. Where would you run then? '

' In the end, yes,' Mr. Miller said, ' but the lamp will detect the presence of a small percentage of marsh gas—as low as one per cent, I believe. The flame elongates and becomes blue and—well, they'd start running *then*, before it went out. That's the whole idea.'

Mr. Herring interrupted.

' The miner now has his cap-lamp to see his way about with. That's electric. He uses it to work with, for it lights up the seam; it's much more convenient. But there's always someone with a Davy Lamp whose duty it is to go round regularly to test for gas.'

' Shall we go? ' said Mr. Miller. ' Now, boys and girls, remember to keep together. We've not got electric lamps in our caps. I don't want to lose any of you. Mr. Herring will lead the way. I will be at the rear. From now on, you and I are to do exactly as he tells us.'

They moved in a body towards the cage. But before they stepped in, Mr. Herring turned to address them.

'Now, boys and girls, this pit is not at present being worked—that is, not the parts where I shall be taking you. It's more or less worked out—that is to say, though there's still quite a lot of good coal down there, there's not enough to make it what we call an economic proposition. Do you know what that means?'

Several voices answered; Mr. Herring called on Annabella to explain.

'It means,' she said, 'it would cost so much to get the coal out, that the pit wouldn't pay its way.'

'That's right,' said Mr. Herring. 'The amount and quality of the coal wouldn't pay for transport and the men's labour, if you know what I mean. So the pit's not in use. But we can't just close it and leave it, because it would then endanger the lives of the men working in other mines around here.'

'How?' somebody asked.

'Well, for one thing,' said Mr. Herring, 'there's this old marsh-gas: it collects in pockets, and it might explode. And again the mine would flood if we left it to itself, and the water would seep out and flood the nearby mines—in fact, we have to keep pumps going all the time. You'll see and hear them.'

'Isn't that expensive?' Annabella asked.

'Of course,' said Mr. Herring. 'But it has to be

done, and that expense has to be met. There are ways and means.'

'I see. But isn't it all rather dangerous ? I still think it would be better to shut this kind of mine down altogether.'

Mr. Herring shook his head.

'The country needs coal,' he said. 'Mines like this just can't be shut down and abandoned without causing the loss of many thousands of tons of best household coal from other mines.'

'But the danger ! Suppose the water seeps because someone forgets about working the pumps, or they stick or something ? '

'The inspectors often come and test for safety— not only to detect the presence of marsh gas and water, but also to see that the roofs won't fall in and trap somebody ; so we needn't be nervous. Are you all ready ? '

'Ay ! ' they all shouted.

They got in the waiting cage and, when the gates were shut and Mr. Herring had touched a lever, they shot down at such a speed that Annabella didn't think she'd ever travelled so fast before, even in a train or an aeroplane. But before she had time to think anything more, they had reached the bottom. The door of the cage opened and they stepped forth, following in a pack on Mr. Herring's heels.

They got in the waiting cage

The Davy Lamps made a line of yellow twinkling lights as they set forth in a crocodile into the darkness, along the galleries of coal. Annabella found it the weirdest and most exciting picture she had ever seen.

From time to time Mr Herring stopped to point out something interesting—the great pumping engines, lumps of black fungus-like stuff on the walls. Once or twice they walked along the borders of deep sinister-looking pools. But, he assured them, these were not dangerous provided you knew where they were.

His laugh went echoing over the water and along the dark glistening corridors. It was very hot. Annabella would have liked to take off the tight-fitting boiler suit, but of course she couldn't. Nobody was working here; all seemed quite deserted.

Mr Herring showed them, just above their heads, how the roof was held up with pit-props. ' Otherwise,' he said, ' it would soon fall down. These wooden props,' he remarked to Mr. Miller, ' are quite out-of-date now; as you know, we mostly use steel arches, which are very strong and last so much longer, but when this old part became worked out, they hadn't yet come into general use.'

Mr. Miller said, ' Don't you think it's time we turned back ? We must have come about a mile.'

Mr. Herring looked at the illuminated dial of his wrist-watch.

'Why, yes!' he said, 'we must have. I lost all sense of time—I was so interested. When I was a lad I used to work in this very section. I used to lie on my back in a hole about three feet high, I was only—twelve—and they gave my butty and me the job because we were small and supple. Couldn't do that now!' he chuckled. 'I guess I weigh fourteen stone.'

'How horrible to work shut in like that!' thought Annabella. She must have breathed the words aloud, because Mr. Herring turned to her and said:

'Oh, it was nothing, missy! We enjoyed it. I was with my dad, and I felt quite the man, a little man, all whipcord muscles, I can assure you. He told me that in his dad's day, or it may have been grandad's, the little children of six and seven used to be sent down the pits to drag the wagons, with a chain round their waists like little animals.' He tapped with his boot the iron rails that ran along the floor of the 'road' as he called the corridor along which they were walking. 'Perhaps some of the poor little kids crawled along these very lines,' he said. 'You see, they could go where even the ponies couldn't.'

'How horrible!' Annabella said, this time aloud.

'No need to worry yourself about such things now, missy!' said Mr. Herring. ''Tis all over and done with, long long ago. It doesn't do to worry too much about the past; though indeed it's a wonder to this day, how Christian ladies and gentlemen could let such things be done and say nothing.'

'They said a good deal,' Mr. Miller said, 'but it was always to the effect that the country would be ruined if the children were barred from working in the mines.'

'I know, I know,' said Mr. Herring. 'But there are other things to bother about now.'

'Tell us!' said Annabella, deciding to make her name as a great reformer, once she knew what was wrong with the world.

'Another day,' Mr. Miller said. 'Mr. Herring, I must take the children back now. Their parents may get anxious.'

'Were you ever trapped in a mine, Mr. Herring?' one of the boys asked.

'I certainly was,' Mr. Herring said.

'Coo; you must have been scared!'

'No, not very, son; you see, as I told you, I was with my dad. We all sang hymns. Lordy, how we sang; we'd have brought the house down at any Eisteddfod with singing like that—Dad and old Blake with their baritone, and Jim Piper with his tenor and the four Taffies and the rest of us harmonising. "Rock of Ages", we sang, and said a few prayers, and then we played cards with a pack one of the men always carried for such an event, and the time passed quickly. But you can't do too much singing ; you use up the air.'

'How long was it ? '

'Forty-eight hours,' Mr. Herring said calmly.

'Two days,' murmured Johnnie. 'Phew ! '

'It was dark for the last twenty-four hours,' Mr. Herring said. 'That was the worst of it. So we couldn't play cards either. The lamps were out, you see, and the batteries of our torches gave out too. So we just went on praying——'

'Gosh, you were brave ! ' Annabella whispered.

'Well, you see, missy,' Mr. Herring said, 'we could hear our mates working to get us out, and we knew they wouldn't give in till they'd rescued us. Of course, the real danger was that there might have been another fall. It's true that by the time they dug through to us, we had next to no air left— so we weren't in much of a shape. But we must go back. This way ! ' He started out on the return journey.

Annabella wasn't sorry, because it was so very hot that she felt stifled, especially, oddly enough, after Mr. Herring's story of being trapped. He turned to say to Mr. Miller :

' There's just one thing more I'd like to show
the children. I think I can find a small pocket
of gas round here : that would interest them.'

He forged ahead and they followed. They had
no idea where they were, or in what direction
they would have to go if Mr. Herring wasn't there
to lead them. He came to a place where the
corridor broadened out into a sort of space, square
like a room. In the middle was one of the dark
pools, which reflected the light of their Davy
Lamps.

Mr. Herring began edging his way along a
narrow ledge in the coal-face above the pool.
Annabella thought, ' What if he falls in ? We'll
never get out,' for she was sure that Mr. Miller,
in spite of his knowledge of coal, had no more idea
of the way back than she had herself.

' Anybody like to come along ? ' Mr. Herring
called out, his voice echoing in the roof. He was
sidling along the ledge, and holding his Davy
Lamp up against the coal-face. ' Come on, lads !
There's no danger ! '

The boys had to go, and Annabella watched,
wondering if she had better go too, or whether
she'd better wait on the edge of the pool and try
to rescue anyone who fell in. As she watched,
suddenly to her horror she saw Mr. Herring's
Davy Lamp go out : and then, one by one, the

He forged ahead and they followed

lamps of all the boys standing on the ledge went out too.

'Back, lads!' Mr. Herring shouted, 'and the rest of you run for it! There's gas here all right!'

'Follow me, children!' Mr. Miller said in a calm, everyday voice, making a bee-line for the exit along the corridor. Annabella glanced down and saw with relief that her own Davy Lamp was still burning, though the flame did seem a little longer, and she thought it had a bluish cone like a Bunsen burner. She waited.

All the boys hopped safely off the ledge, and joined the rest of the party with Mr. Miller. Lastly came Johnnie and Mr. Herring.

'There was a little more gas than I bargained for,' he said. 'Well, never mind. There's no harm done.' He was rather out of breath, Annabella noticed, but then, of course, he was rather fat.

CHAPTER 7

A FALSE ALARM

I

DURING the next few weeks Mr. Miller did not fail
to give them a good deal of instruction about coal
and coal-mines; and the other masters and
mistresses, knowing of the expedition, also slipped
in information about coal whenever they could,
and drew pictures on the board. But all this
would have meant little to Annabella if she had
not been down to the bottom of a mine and seen
for herself what it was like. Sometimes she woke
at night with a feeling of suffocation and dreamed
she was down there and that there was gas, and
when she woke up it seemed to her she could still
smell the queer dry smell of the coal, and her
heart would beat fast. . . .

Out of all the instruction on coal that she received,
Annabella remembered only a few facts, and these
were told her in conversation with Mr. Williams,
whose father had been a colliery manager. Mr.
Williams said that the coal in this country is got
from pits far deeper than those in the United States:
he said that the coal there mostly comes from pits

less than a thousand feet deep, whereas here it comes from pits between fifteen hundred and four thousand feet deep.

He looked over the top of his newspaper and saw Annabella's expression.

' Yes, I know,' he said. ' It's not easy for you to visualise four thousand feet, especially when you have to think of them standing on end ; but if you can think of walking three quarters of a mile and then set that distance upright, or—let me see—let us think of some building in London.'

' What about St. Paul's ? ' said Theo.

' St. Paul's. Theo, get the encyclopaedia and look up the height of St. Paul's.'

Theo did so.

' It says here,' she said, ' that St. Paul's is three hundred and sixty-five feet from the ground to the top of the cross.'

' That's right,' said Annabella.

' You don't mean to say you knew ? '

' Of course,' said Annabella. ' When I was taken to visit St. Paul's the guide told us the height, and he said the way to remember it was easy—it was the same number of feet as there are days in the year.'

' So it is,' said Theo.

' Well, well,' said Mr. Williams. ' I must re-member that. Now then, when I tell you the pit you went down is ten times that depth, you get some idea of the depth from which we get our coal.'

Annabella thought of the time when her uncle and aunt took her to visit St. Paul's, and they had gone up to the Whispering Gallery which runs round the dome on the inside; and then she thought of looking down to the floor and how far away it seemed; and then she thought what it would be like to slide down from that height on a rope; and that gave her a good idea of the depth to which they had gone down in the cage. Ten times the height of St. Paul's! She would have something to talk about when she got back.

2

Three weeks after their visit, there was an accident in that mine; it was not in the pit they had visited but in a nearby one where the men were still working; there had been a fall of rock from one of the roofs.

Instantly there was terror in the village, and everybody rushed to the pit-head. When Annabella and the girls came home to tea they had already heard the news, which had spread like wild-fire. But by that time everything was over, and all the people had gone home.

It happened to be the night for their Ambulance Class, and there Annabella heard the whole story from one of the Ambulance Brigade men who had gone to the pit thinking he might be needed.

The fall of rock had not been serious, and nobody had been badly hurt, so that the help of the First Aiders was not called for. Mr. Harrison, the Captain of the Number One team, seemed rather disappointed, but he explained :

' Of course, every mine has a group of its own trained rescue-workers on call in case of accidents, and lots of the other chaps are First Aiders too, but we were able to deal with a man who had crushed his hand when loading one of the underground trucks ; and Mr. Hawkins was able to dress the wound before the regular man arrived on the scene.

Annabella and Theo went along to call for Daisy and Johnnie. Wilf opened the door.

' Come in,' he said, more affably than usual. ' I was longing to see you ; to look at you both.'

Annabella glanced at Theo : she could smell danger.

' I wanted to see for myself,' Wilf said, ' exactly how two very disappointed girls look.'

' Disappointed ? ' Annabella said. ' What do you mean ? '

They were by now standing in the kitchen,

where Mr. and Mrs. Stott were sitting on either side of the fire.

' I've seen,' Wilf said, ' one picture of disappointment.' He waved his hand towards Johnnie, who with Daisy was sitting at the table doing his homework.

' Shut up, Wilf,' Johnnie said, standing up. ' I thought of coming to see you this evening. Let's go before it gets any later.'

' Wait a minute,' Annabella said. ' I want to know exactly what Wilf is getting at.'

' Well, weren't you disappointed, as First Aiders,' Wilf said sneeringly, ' that nobody was badly hurt at the colliery this morning ? No blood ; no broken bones.'

' Hush, dear,' Mrs. Stott said ; ' that's not a nice thing to say, and it's not at all funny either.'

' But, Mother, they love to help people,' Wilf said. ' Their motto is "Pro Humanitate"—For the Service of Mankind. And how can they be of service to mankind if nothing goes wrong ? Therefore they're bound to be disappointed that nobody got bashed about.'

Mr. Stott laughed behind his paper.

Annabella said :

' It might be a good thing if some people saved their breath to . . .' She stopped, not wanting to be as rude as she felt.

'To cool their porridge!' Wilf said, with pretended politeness. At this Annabella lost her temper and said :

'No ; to blow their own—bugle.'

Wilf looked furious. Mrs. Stott knitted very hard, and Mr. Stott crackled his newspaper.

'You shouldn't have said that, Annabella,' Johnnie said as he walked with her up the street.

'I couldn't help it,' Annabella said. 'It seems to me Wilf gets too much of his own way. His father and mother encourage him. They're too silly for words.'

'And now he'll never play the bugle again,' Johnnie said.

'That 'll be a mercy,' remarked Daisy.

'What does Mr. Stott do?' Annabella said, because she couldn't think of anything else to say, if she were not to annoy Johnnie.

'He's a sort of paymaster or something,' Johnnie said. 'He goes to the bank on Saturdays and collects the money for the men's pay and takes it up to the colliery.'

'So that's why he has a car.'

'Yes.'

'And that's what makes him—rather proud.'

'I suppose so,' Johnnie said. 'But I don't think he's at all proud.'

CHAPTER 8

THE RESCUE

I

IT was a Saturday morning.

The day was fine and bright, though rather cold. Annabella, Theo, Johnnie and Daisy were again walking on the mountain. This had become a regular excursion for them on every fine Saturday ; they usually went in the afternoon, but Johnnie came only in the mornings when the Melintre Rugby First Fifteen were playing at home. On those afternoons he watched the match, and he wanted the girls to come too.

Annabella and Theo used to go sometimes in the hope of being called upon to set a broken collar bone, but nobody ever got injured. Daisy and Julie wouldn't go : they said the game bored them, and that it was so cold standing about. However it meant that if Johnnie was to come with them on their walks, they had to go on Saturday morning.

Another member of the party was Roger, the Williams' little white dog, who barked furiously at first, but was quite good once they got on to the mountain.

They had been up as far as The Pimple and were on the way back. They could see, from the path that ran round the mountain, the whole of the village of Treglo with its double row of houses; the railway station and the railway line winding up the valley towards the coal-tips shaped like pyramids, and at the foot of the mountain, following its curve, they could see the main road.

It was not a very wide main road; in fact, Annabella would have called it a country lane a few months ago. The hedges were high, and in places the road was too narrow for cars to pass, or at any rate for a car to pass a lorry; and so there were places cut at the sides where a car or lorry could pull in and wait for another car or lorry to pass.

The path on which they were coming down the mountain wound right round it in a spiral, so that at times they were out of sight of the village and the road. They were about half-way down when they came round for about the third time and looking down on to the main road below, they saw something new.

Drawn up in one of the 'lay-bys' there was a small car; and lying on his back in the middle of the road there was a man with three other men grouped round him. The three men were not doing anything: they were just standing with their

hands in their pockets, staring back down the road
as if waiting for something.

'An accident!' Annabella shouted, and she left
the path and went plunging down the mountain
side. She leaped over tufts of grass and brambles,
and it was a wonder how she kept on her feet,
because the hillside was steep here. Johnnie went
plunging after her. Theo followed more slowly.
Daisy stayed where she was.

When Annabella reached the men in the road,
they all turned round in amazement. They had
just heard her coming, because some small stones
which she scattered as she ran, arrived before her.
She had the strange idea that they were not very
pleased to see her.

She was breathless. She gasped as she reached
them.

'Is that man badly hurt?'

They looked down at the man on the road.
One of them said:

'No, miss, not really-like.'

Another of the men pushed the other two back
and faced her.

'Then why,' Annabella said, 'is he lying there?
It's dangerous. Things whizz past here. What's
happened? Hasn't there been an accident?'

By now Johnnie had reached them.

The leader of the party said:

'Of course there's been an accident. This fellow's broken his hip.'

'Then we'll examine him,' Annabella said in a business-like way. 'We're First Aiders, so there'll be lots we can do. Would you like one of us to fetch a doctor ?   Or will one of you go ? '

'No——' said the man.

'What about the ambulance ? '

'We've seen to all that,' the man said irritably. 'Now will you please clear out and leave us alone ? We don't need any help.'

'Come on, Annabella,' Johnnie said, looking embarrassed, touching her elbow. Theo had now joined them, and they all walked off together.

'That's funny,' said Annabella. 'I wonder why they wouldn't let me examine him.'

'Because,' said Johnnie, with a broad grin, 'you said we were First Aiders. Wilf's father says those words terrify anybody who's been hurt in an accident, and should never be used.'

Theo and Annabella both began to protest. Then Johnnie exclaimed :

'I say ! I thought we were told, as if it were a law of the Medes and Persians, that if a chap had a fractured hip, his foot lay on its side.'

'Of course,' said Theo ; 'it always does.'

'Well,' said Johnnie, 'either there's something wrong with our teaching, as Wilf always says there is, or else that man didn't have a fractured hip.'

' What makes you say that ? ' Annabella said.

' Because both his feet were pointing upwards. I noticed it particularly, because I thought " His shoes are brand-new "—the price was stamped on the two soles. They were those very pointed shoes.'

' Johnnie, you're right,' Annabella said. She stopped walking. ' I knew it ! Those men are up to something : I could feel it. That man on the ground was only pretending to be hurt. That's why they wouldn't let us look at him ! I *knew* it was queer at the time. The foot *always* lies on the side, and you can tell that to Wilf.'

' Should we go back ? Or ring the police ? There *is* something funny going on, Annabella.'

' No,' Annabella said; ' there may not be time to get anyone, and who'd believe us ? Whatever it is those men are up to, it's due to happen quite soon—else the man wouldn't lie in the road *now*. If we waste time rushing off to the call-box and explaining to the sergeant—who may be out— and he has to get to the spot, it 'll take ages to explain where it is, and everything may be over. I suggest we climb on to the hill—*here*—and lie in wait just above them and watch. Then we'll be in a position to *do* something ourselves. Theo, could you climb back to where Daisy is waiting,

and get Roger ? He stayed with her—but he might
be useful ; those teeth of his and that awful bark.
But don't *let* him bark till the right moment
comes.   He knows you.'

' Roger won't bark,' Theo said, ' if I tell him not
to. And if I say " Bark ! " he'll bark. He's a very
intelligent dog—more intelligent than many human
beings.'

She cast a glance at Johnnie. He knew she was
referring to his friend, Wilf Stott, but he said
nothing. He followed Annabella through a hole
in the hedge at the side of the road, and back to a
place immediately above where the men were
standing.

They crouched behind some gorse-bushes at a
spot from which they could run straight down to
the stationary car.

2

The man who had been lying in the road suddenly got up and stood with the other three men
in the 'lay-by '.

Johnnie nudged Annabella :

' Fractured hip—my foot ! ' he said.

' S-sh ! ' said Annabella.

Several cars, vans and lorries passed along the
road, but took no notice of the four men, except
for one lorry-driver who shouted out :

They crouched behind some gorse-bushes

' Want any help, mates ? '

' No ! ' they shouted back.

Then they put their heads together again, but
Annabella and Johnnie could not hear a word they
were saying.

Then a man came up on a motor-bike, he said
quite loudly :

' Your pigeon is the next but one,' and then he
rode on again.

A car passed.

The man who'd been lying in the road went on
to the roadway again and lay down in a crumpled
position. The other three smeared some dust on
his face and then stood watching over him.

Presently a small car appeared. It drew up as
it reached the man lying in the road, and the
driver got out.

The driver was—Mr. Stott.

3

Theo had now joined her friends behind the
gorse-bush, with Roger, who lay perfectly still
with his tongue hanging out.

' That's Wilf's father,' Theo said.

' S-sh ! ' said Annabella.

Mr. Stott, who looked almost as white as his own
collar, went to look at the man lying on the road.

'I'm afraid,' they heard him stammer, 'I'm no use to you; you'll have to have a doctor—Wilf! What about your doing something?'

Wilf stepped out of the passenger's seat; he too crossed over to look at the supposedly injured man.

Then everything began to happen at once. One of the three men turned suddenly and seized Mr. Stott's arms and pinned them behind his back; the 'injured' man jumped up and grabbed Wilf, while the other two ran towards Mr. Stott's car as fast as if they had been trying to beat the record. Their heads vanished inside the car. Then one of them yelled: 'Here it is!' waving a canvas bag he had dragged off the rear seat of the Stotts' car. Mr. Stott might turn pale at the sight of blood, but the sight of the canvas bag being dragged from his car drove all the colour back into his face. With a roar to Wilf to free himself, he twisted and struggled and fought like a tiger in a net. But, though Wilf and Mr. Stott struggled hard, the men were too strong for them, and they could not get away. And at that moment Annabella acted.

'Now!' she yelled, and all three children jumped from their hiding-place into the road. 'Tell him to bark!' Annabella said to Theo. 'Make him sound like a bloodhound!'

'Bark, Roger! Bark, bark!' Theo said.
Roger barked.

The men were so surprised at the sight of the three children that for an instant they relaxed their grip, and in that instant Wilf and Mr. Stott were able to struggle free. But the man with the canvas bag still held it.

' Come on, Jim ! ' one of the others shouted to him, and they all turned and ran towards their own car—all except Jim ; he could not, because Roger made for him and caught him by the trouser-leg. Roger, happier than he had ever been before in his life, was growling and tugging, and all the men were shouting. One of them had started the engine of their car, when a piece of the trouser-leg came away in Roger's teeth, and the man called Jim, still holding the canvas bag, was free. He was in the car before Roger had time to recover from his surprise.

The men might all have got away, at any rate for the time being, if Annabella hadn't said to Mr. Stott :

' Mr. Stott, drive your car across the road. They won't dare to bash into it.'

And Wilf said :

' Yes, Dad, that's right,' and when his father didn't move, Wilf jumped into the driving seat and swung their car at a right angle so that the other car couldn't get past. Then before the men had time to reverse and make off in the other direction, a lorry came along and nearly went into them. The driver got out and strode up to Wilf and shouted at him for having nearly caused a serious accident.

'It wouldn't have mattered, driver,' Annabella interrupted coolly. 'You see, we are all First Aiders.' And then whilst he stared at her in amazement, Mr. Stott came up and explained all that had happened, and enlisted the lorry-driver's help. The lorry-driver gave it with a will.

4

The four men were arrested and tried and sent to prison for having attempted a highway robbery. It turned out that they had known that Mr. Stott went to the bank regularly on Saturday mornings just before eleven, and then drove up the valley to the colliery with the money ; the robbery had been planned for some time, and the robbers had been watching Mr. Stott so that they should know all his movements. Finally, their plan had been to make him stop and get out of his car to attend to the accident they had faked ; but their elaborate plans were foiled by the children. The Judge mentioned all this in Court and thanked Theo, Annabella and Johnnie for their public-spirited action. He dwelt on their keen observation in noticing the foot that pointed upwards when it should have been lying on its side.

' It was such a little clue if you didn't know about it, but such a telling one if you did, as the prisoners are now realising.   It is a good thing,' he then went on to say, ' when our boys and girls realise at an early age that they should help to see that the laws of the country are kept.   Our police force is only a small one to deal with the criminal class ; and therefore it is necessary that every citizen, young and old, should help to maintain law and order.

' Also, from the point of view of the prisoners, we can say that these young people have acted for their good ; for if these children had not intervened, the prisoners might have been tempted to use greater violence, and they might have been here on an even more serious charge.   Remember, violence leads to greater violence, and when a criminal feels that his prey is escaping, he may be led on to ... but, however, mercifully, that did not happen.'

The Judge paused, and folded his hands and looked at the Court over the top of his glasses :

' I understand,' he said, ' that these young people are all members of the organisation known as the Venerable Order of St. John of Jerusalem, an ancient Order of Chivalry founded by good Christian men to protect the weak and suffering.

I gather they learn many useful subjects, not only First Aid but also subjects which are useful at all times, including good citizenship. I commend them, in that they have begun at this early age to take the right road—that of service to their fellowmen.'

Annabella could not resist a glance at Wilf Stott, who had been giving evidence and was now sitting with them.

He looked rather red.

CHAPTER 9

THE RETURN JOURNEY

I

IN the middle of the spring term, a letter came to say that the work on their London school was now finished; and that Annabella, Johnnie and Daisy could go home and be ready to start the new term there.

They were glad in one way, sorry in others, as they went round saying goodbye to their friends, for they had made many friends, and the weeks seemed to have flown past. Annabella was especially sorry to say goodbye to the Williams family who had been so kind to her.

2

When at last they were sitting in the express train bound for London, Annabella thought of all the things that had happened since they had passed this way before. Johnnie and Daisy looked thoughtful too. When they ran into the Severn Tunnel Johnnie looked at his wrist-watch, and when they came out at the other end he said to Annabella:

'It only took four and three-quarter minutes; you said " seven and a half ". Remember ? '

'I remember,' Annabella said, looking a little bit uncomfortable. 'I expect the book where I read that was out of date : the trains run faster now. Everybody knows that,' she added brightly.

On the other side of the Tunnel they noticed a small station called ' Coal Pit Heath '. They all ran to look out of the window.'

'I wonder where the coal-pit is,' Johnnie said.

'That was what I was thinking,' Annabella said. 'I don't see any signs of it, do you ? '

This was another chance to say 'Remember?' and to go back over the adventure in the mine, when the Davy Lamps went out.

3

'Of course I'm longing to see Aunt Meg and Uncle Bob,' Annabella said, ' but I shall miss the Williams.' Then she glanced at Johnnie and said, 'I expect you were pretty sorry to say goodbye to the Stotts.'

'I was,' Johnnie said shortly.

After a while, Annabella said :

'Wilf hasn't joined the St. John yet, has he ? Does he still play the bugle ? '

'No,' said Johnnie; 'the neighbours complained, so he had to give it up.'

' Then he won't join ?   Ever ? '

' He'll join,' Johnnie said, ' when the right time comes.   He doesn't need to be a bugler.   You see, he'll be sixteen in August, so next winter he could join the Adult Class under Mr. Herring.'

' Oh, hooray ! ' Annabella said.   ' Don't look cross, Johnnie : Wilf isn't here to get mad at me.'

' Wilf wasn't ever really mad with you.   He said you'd got quite good points, but that you got his goat somehow.   He is going to join now.   He told me so, but he made me promise not to tell you till we'd got home.'

' Well,' Annabella said, ' if he's made up his mind, nobody 'll be able to talk him out of it. I will say this for Wilf—he knows his own mind.'

4

As the train neared Reading, the railway lines ran for a while alongside the road, and they watched the traffic, hoping that the train would go faster than the cars.   Annabella saw a man on a motor-bike.

' That reminds me,' she said.   ' Johnnie, you know that man on the motor-bike, the one who came past and told the others that Mr. Stott's car was coming ? '

' Yes,' said Johnnie,   ' Wasn't it a shame that

they found him Not Guilty ? He was just as bad
as the others.'

' He was,' agreed Annabella, ' but they couldn't
prove it. He said he was just riding past as it
happened, and in English law everybody's innocent
until he's proved guilty.'

' I know,' Johnnie said, ' but we both gave
evidence against him. We both—we all—heard
what he said, and you and I picked him out at the
identification parade.'

' That's not the point,' said Annabella. ' The
point was, the police couldn't *prove* that he'd taken
part in the actual attempted robbery.'

' Huh ! ' Johnnie said. ' So I suppose he can
go off and take a hand in committing some other
crime.'

' No,' Annabella said ; ' that's just what I was
going to tell you. The police are going to bring
another charge against him.'

' Can they ? '

' Yes. A charge of driving without stopping
after an accident, and of failing to report it.'
Johnnie looked at her.

' You mean . . .? '

Annabella shook her head.

' No, not the fake accident, but a real one—
he was the same man who knocked you and Wilf
down that night when you were riding the bike.'

' Gosh !   How do you know ? '

' One of the men in court recognised him.   He
—a man from Treglo—was in the Treglo Arms
when you were knocked down, and he came out
before the man on the motor-bike rode away.   He
saw his face distinctly in the headlights of an
oncoming car, and he reported this to the police.
So the police arrested the motor cyclist, after all,
just as he was leaving the Court after the verdict.'

' How do you know, Annabella ? '

' Mr. Williams told me just before I left.   He
says the police will ask for the biggest possible
penalty.   He said too that it showed that the
police are like the elephant—they never forget.'

All three laughed.